THE FIRST

**90**

**DAYS**

AFTER

BIRTH

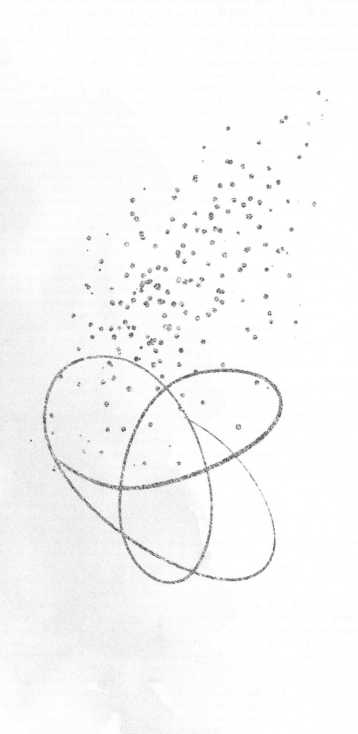

# THE FIRST
# 90
# DAYS
# AFTER
# BIRTH

*A Self-Care Journal*

## FOR FIRST-TIME MOMS

KIM BURRIS, LMFT

**R**

**ROCKRIDGE
PRESS**

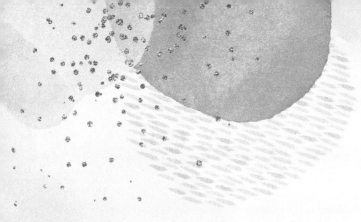

For general information on our other products and services or to obtain technical support, please contact our Customer Care Department within the United States at (866) 744-2665, or outside the United States at (510) 253-0500.

Rockridge Press publishes its books in a variety of electronic and print formats. Some content that appears in print may not be available in electronic books, and vice versa.

TRADEMARKS: Rockridge Press and the Rockridge Press logo are trademarks or registered trademarks of Callisto Media Inc. and/or its affiliates, in the United States and other countries, and may not be used without written permission. All other trademarks are the property of their respective owners. Rockridge Press is not associated with any product or vendor mentioned in this book.

Interior and Cover Designer: Linda Snorina
Art Producer: Megan Baggott
Editor: Brian Sweeting
Production Editor: Mia Moran
Production Manager: Holly Haydash

Illustrations: Veris Studio/Creative Market
Author photo courtesy of Theresa Winslow

ISBN: Print 978-1-64876-702-9
R0

This journal belongs to:

_____

# Introduction

Hello, beauty! Welcome to the wild world of motherhood! I'm Kim Burris, licensed holistic psychotherapist and mother of two young boys. I have been immersed in the worlds of psychology and spirituality for over 20 years and believe wholeheartedly that self-care is not a luxury but a necessity on our path to wholeness.

I know firsthand how easy it can be to lose your footing in this new world and stumble under the weight of exhaustion, feeling overwhelmed, and mom guilt. The struggle is real. In the chaos of motherhood, I want you to know that learning to practice self-care in this phase of your life is not only possible but imperative. I have helped hundreds of women learn the art of nurturing themselves, and I'm here to help you, too.

For the next 90 days, I'll be supporting you in crafting a self-care routine that is manageable and deeply nourishing to your whole self: mind, body, heart, and spirit. I want you to know that whatever struggles you face, you aren't facing them alone. Together we will weave a golden thread that will keep you connected to yourself and the infinite wisdom that lives within so that no matter the challenge, you can always find your way back home.

# A CHANGING TIME

You made it—you've crossed over to the mystical fourth trimester. I know prioritizing yourself can sometimes feel like one more thing on your new and endless to-do list, but hold on to yourself, mama. These first 90 days are the ideal time to create self-care habits that will help you become the mom you want to be. I invite you to be gentle with yourself as well as persistent in carving out time for daily self-care.

*Postpartum* literally means "after childbirth," and there are a heck of a lot of challenges and stressors to navigate in this phase of life. Honor your feelings. It's definitely not supposed to be rainbows and unicorns every day. This job is hard. If you are experiencing anxiety, fear, unwanted or intrusive thoughts, rage, anger, hopelessness, or despair, please know that you are not alone. And you do not have to meet the diagnostic criteria for a postpartum mood disorder such as postpartum anxiety or postpartum depression to get help. If the weight of motherhood feels too heavy, please reach out now to a licensed mental health professional and/or your primary care physician for support. Don't wait. And while this book is not a replacement for therapy, medication, or medical treatments, I do hope it will inspire and encourage you to take exquisite care of yourself today and always.

So, mama, are you ready? This motherhood journey truly is a marathon, not a sprint, so be kind as you learn to care for yourself and your precious babe. Some days will be full of ease, bliss, and contentment. Some days will be harrowing, exhausting, and overwhelming. As you take the time to build healthy habits, you will create a pattern of self-reflection and self-care to sustain you on even the hardest of days.

You got this. And please don't forget: You made a baby, and you birthed a baby. You are truly made of magic.

# HOW TO USE THIS JOURNAL

This journal was created for you to thrive, not just survive, in this precious and precarious time. For the next 90 days, I invite you to commit to the practice of daily self-care. Each day you'll find a checklist of simple, actionable ways to care for yourself along with an inspirational journal prompt and space to write. These were designed with you—a busy new mom—in mind. Take as much or as little time as you can find each day to practice. And, yes, even one minute of self-care counts.

Now, let's get you set up to thrive! Take a moment to think about why you chose this book and what you hope to receive from cultivating a self-care practice. Perhaps it's to gain new tools and skills for this challenging phase of life or to learn to be more patient, kind, and compassionate with yourself.

Now think about when and where you can practice. I suggest doing it during your baby's first nap of the day in a cozy location such as your bed or outside (just bring the baby monitor). Aim to take your self-care time every day when this event happens.

And don't forget to store your journal somewhere visible and easy to access like on your nightstand, near the changing table, or even on the bathroom counter.

Write down your plan here.

I'm practicing self-care to cultivate more (self-compassion, self-love, patience, etc.) _____

_____

I will practice every day when (the baby naps, before bedtime, etc.) _____

_____

I will take my self-care time (in my bed, on the deck, etc.) _____

_____

   Take a moment now to visualize yourself picking up this book tomorrow. Take a deep breath and see yourself checking off some items on the self-care checklist, reading the journal prompt, writing a few things down, and then setting the book back down. Notice what it feels like to take a few minutes just for yourself.

   See? You got this. If you miss a day, it's all good; just pick up where you left off. You can't do it wrong because there's no right way to do self-care. The invitation is to show up, love yourself the best way that you can, and let yourself be supported, mama. You are not alone. I'll see you tomorrow.

# DAY 1

Taking time every day to focus on yourself with loving care and attention is a gift. What are you hoping to experience and gain on this 90-day self-care journey?

_____

_____

_____

_____

_____

_____

_____

_____

_____

_____

_____

_____

_____

_____

_____

_____

# SELF-CARE CHECKLIST

*Check the ways you've taken care of*
*(or intend to take care of) yourself today:*

## REST DEEPLY

○ Prioritize nighttime sleep

○ Nap when the baby naps at least once a day

## EAT MINDFULLY

○ Nourish yourself with healthy meals and snacks

○ Drink plenty of water

## HONOR RELATIONSHIPS

○ Connect with your partner, a close friend, or a relative

○ Text or call a friend

## MOVE YOUR BEAUTIFUL BODY

○ Stretch in bed

○ Practice gentle yoga or Pilates

## BE KIND TO YOURSELF

○ Shower and brush teeth and hair

○ Open a window, breathe in fresh air, and smile

○ Practice meditation or breathwork

○ Pray, sing, or dance

○ Other: _____

## FEEL YOUR FEELINGS

○ Today I feel _____

## ASK FOR SUPPORT

*Today I could use help with . . .*

○ Holding the baby while I shower or rest

○ Preparing food

○ Laundry and cleaning

○ Other: _____

Today I will ask for help from _____

# DAY 2

Honor your birth story by writing down what happened. What was the hardest part? What was the best part? *(If a lot of feelings come up here, that's totally normal and expected; please talk more with a loved one.)*

_____

_____

_____

_____

_____

_____

_____

_____

_____

_____

_____

_____

_____

_____

_____

_____

_____

_____

_____

_____

_____

_____

# SELF-CARE CHECKLIST

*Check the ways you've taken care of*
*(or intend to take care of) yourself today:*

## REST DEEPLY

○ Prioritize nighttime sleep

○ Nap when the baby naps at least once a day

## EAT MINDFULLY

○ Nourish yourself with healthy meals and snacks

○ Drink plenty of water

## HONOR RELATIONSHIPS

○ Connect with your partner, a close friend, or a relative

○ Text or call a friend

## MOVE YOUR BEAUTIFUL BODY

○ Stretch in bed

○ Practice gentle yoga or Pilates

## BE KIND TO YOURSELF

○ Shower and brush teeth and hair

○ Practice meditation or breathwork

○ Open a window, breathe in fresh air, and smile

○ Pray, sing, or dance

○ Other: _____

## FEEL YOUR FEELINGS

○ Today I feel _____

## ASK FOR SUPPORT

*Today I could use help with . . .*

○ Holding the baby while I shower or rest

○ Laundry and cleaning

○ Other: _____

○ Preparing food

Today I will ask for help from _____

# DAY 3

Reach out to the important people in your life. Who would you like support from? Who can you call to come over and help, or talk to that would feel encouraging and supportive?

_____

_____

_____

_____

_____

_____

_____

_____

_____

_____

_____

_____

_____

_____

_____

_____

_____

_____

_____

# SELF-CARE CHECKLIST

*Check the ways you've taken care of
(or intend to take care of) yourself today:*

## REST DEEPLY

○ Prioritize nighttime sleep

○ Nap when the baby naps at least once a day

## EAT MINDFULLY

○ Nourish yourself with healthy meals and snacks

○ Drink plenty of water

## HONOR RELATIONSHIPS

○ Connect with your partner, a close friend, or a relative

○ Text or call a friend

## MOVE YOUR BEAUTIFUL BODY

○ Stretch in bed

○ Practice gentle yoga or Pilates

## BE KIND TO YOURSELF

○ Shower and brush teeth and hair

○ Open a window, breathe in fresh air, and smile

○ Practice meditation or breathwork

○ Pray, sing, or dance

○ Other: _____

## FEEL YOUR FEELINGS

○ Today I feel _____

## ASK FOR SUPPORT

*Today I could use help with . . .*

○ Holding the baby while I shower or rest

○ Preparing food

○ Laundry and cleaning

○ Other: _____

Today I will ask for help from _____

# DAY 4

Your beautiful postpartum body looks and feels different than it did before birth. Write down five things about your body that you are grateful for.

1. _____

_____

_____

2. _____

_____

_____

3. _____

_____

_____

4. _____

_____

_____

5. _____

_____

_____

# SELF-CARE CHECKLIST

*Check the ways you've taken care of
(or intend to take care of) yourself today:*

## REST DEEPLY

○ Prioritize nighttime sleep

○ Nap when the baby naps at least once a day

## EAT MINDFULLY

○ Nourish yourself with healthy meals and snacks

○ Drink plenty of water

## HONOR RELATIONSHIPS

○ Connect with your partner, a close friend, or a relative

○ Text or call a friend

## MOVE YOUR BEAUTIFUL BODY

○ Stretch in bed

○ Practice gentle yoga or Pilates

## BE KIND TO YOURSELF

○ Shower and brush teeth and hair

○ Open a window, breathe in fresh air, and smile

○ Practice meditation or breathwork

○ Pray, sing, or dance

○ Other: _____

## FEEL YOUR FEELINGS

○ Today I feel _____

## ASK FOR SUPPORT

*Today I could use help with . . .*

○ Holding the baby while I shower or rest

○ Preparing food

○ Laundry and cleaning

○ Other: _____

Today I will ask for help from _____

Reflect on your pregnancy experience. How did your expectations compare to reality? Would you do anything differently if you could do it over again?

_____

_____

_____

_____

_____

_____

_____

_____

_____

_____

_____

_____

_____

_____

_____

_____

_____

_____

_____

_____

_____

# SELF-CARE CHECKLIST

*Check the ways you've taken care of*
*(or intend to take care of) yourself today:*

## REST DEEPLY

○ Prioritize nighttime sleep

○ Nap when the baby naps at least once a day

## EAT MINDFULLY

○ Nourish yourself with healthy meals and snacks

○ Drink plenty of water

## HONOR RELATIONSHIPS

○ Connect with your partner, a close friend, or a relative

○ Text or call a friend

## MOVE YOUR BEAUTIFUL BODY

○ Stretch in bed

○ Practice gentle yoga or Pilates

## BE KIND TO YOURSELF

○ Shower and brush teeth and hair

○ Open a window, breathe in fresh air, and smile

○ Practice meditation or breathwork

○ Pray, sing, or dance

○ Other: _____

## FEEL YOUR FEELINGS

○ Today I feel _____

## ASK FOR SUPPORT

*Today I could use help with . . .*

○ Holding the baby while I shower or rest

○ Preparing food

○ Laundry and cleaning

○ Other: _____

Today I will ask for help from _____

# DAY 6

Make a list of all the things you've done so far today and marvel at what you've already accomplished. *(Yes, drinking water, changing diapers, having a snack, and going to the bathroom count!)*

# SELF-CARE CHECKLIST

*Check the ways you've taken care of
(or intend to take care of) yourself today:*

## REST DEEPLY

○ Prioritize nighttime sleep

○ Nap when the baby naps at least once a day

## EAT MINDFULLY

○ Nourish yourself with healthy meals and snacks

○ Drink plenty of water

## HONOR RELATIONSHIPS

○ Connect with your partner, a close friend, or a relative

○ Text or call a friend

## MOVE YOUR BEAUTIFUL BODY

○ Stretch in bed

○ Practice gentle yoga or Pilates

## BE KIND TO YOURSELF

○ Shower and brush teeth and hair

○ Open a window, breathe in fresh air, and smile

○ Practice meditation or breathwork

○ Pray, sing, or dance

○ Other: _____

## FEEL YOUR FEELINGS

○ Today I feel _____

## ASK FOR SUPPORT

*Today I could use help with . . .*

○ Holding the baby while I shower or rest

○ Preparing food

○ Laundry and cleaning

○ Other: _____

Today I will ask for help from _____

# DAY 7

Let yourself rest. Your body needs time to recover and for your organs to begin moving back into place. What feelings come up as you invite yourself to move at a slower pace of life?

_____

_____

_____

_____

_____

_____

_____

_____

_____

_____

_____

_____

_____

_____

_____

_____

_____

_____

# SELF-CARE CHECKLIST

*Check the ways you've taken care of*
*(or intend to take care of) yourself today:*

## REST DEEPLY

○ Prioritize nighttime sleep

○ Nap when the baby naps at least once a day

## EAT MINDFULLY

○ Nourish yourself with healthy meals and snacks

○ Drink plenty of water

## HONOR RELATIONSHIPS

○ Connect with your partner, a close friend, or a relative

○ Text or call a friend

## MOVE YOUR BEAUTIFUL BODY

○ Stretch in bed

○ Practice gentle yoga or Pilates

## BE KIND TO YOURSELF

○ Shower and brush teeth and hair

○ Open a window, breathe in fresh air, and smile

○ Practice meditation or breathwork

○ Pray, sing, or dance

○ Other: _____

## FEEL YOUR FEELINGS

○ Today I feel _____

## ASK FOR SUPPORT

*Today I could use help with . . .*

○ Holding the baby while I shower or rest

○ Preparing food

○ Laundry and cleaning

○ Other: _____

Today I will ask for help from _____

# DAY 8

You've made it to the second week of motherhood! Woo-hoo!
What's the most surprising part of being a new mom?

_____

_____

_____

_____

_____

_____

_____

_____

_____

_____

_____

_____

_____

_____

_____

_____

_____

_____

_____

# SELF-CARE CHECKLIST

*Check the ways you've taken care of*
*(or intend to take care of) yourself today:*

## REST DEEPLY

○ Prioritize nighttime sleep

○ Nap when the baby naps at least once a day

## EAT MINDFULLY

○ Nourish yourself with healthy meals and snacks

○ Drink plenty of water

## HONOR RELATIONSHIPS

○ Connect with your partner, a close friend, or a relative

○ Text or call a friend

## MOVE YOUR BEAUTIFUL BODY

○ Stretch in bed

○ Practice gentle yoga or Pilates

## BE KIND TO YOURSELF

○ Shower and brush teeth and hair

○ Open a window, breathe in fresh air, and smile

○ Practice meditation or breathwork

○ Pray, sing, or dance

○ Other: _____

## FEEL YOUR FEELINGS

○ Today I feel _____

## ASK FOR SUPPORT

*Today I could use help with . . .*

○ Holding the baby while I shower or rest

○ Preparing food

○ Laundry and cleaning

○ Other: _____

Today I will ask for help from _____

# DAY 9

Check in with your mental state today. What is going on in your mind? Some chaos or calm? Endless chatter or spaciousness? Put it all down here as a way to let it go.

_____

_____

_____

_____

_____

_____

_____

_____

_____

_____

_____

_____

_____

_____

_____

_____

_____

# SELF-CARE CHECKLIST

*Check the ways you've taken care of
(or intend to take care of) yourself today:*

## REST DEEPLY

- ○ Prioritize nighttime sleep
- ○ Nap when the baby naps at least once a day

## EAT MINDFULLY

- ○ Nourish yourself with healthy meals and snacks
- ○ Drink plenty of water

## HONOR RELATIONSHIPS

- ○ Connect with your partner, a close friend, or a relative
- ○ Text or call a friend

## MOVE YOUR BEAUTIFUL BODY

- ○ Stretch in bed
- ○ Practice gentle yoga or Pilates

## BE KIND TO YOURSELF

- ○ Shower and brush teeth and hair
- ○ Practice meditation or breathwork
- ○ Open a window, breathe in fresh air, and smile
- ○ Pray, sing, or dance
- ○ Other: _____

## FEEL YOUR FEELINGS

- ○ Today I feel _____

## ASK FOR SUPPORT

*Today I could use help with . . .*

- ○ Holding the baby while I shower or rest
- ○ Laundry and cleaning
- ○ Other: _____
- ○ Preparing food

Today I will ask for help from _____

# DAY 10

How do you feel when you think about self-care? Excited? Relieved? Annoyed? What did self-care look like before motherhood? What does it mean to you now?

_____

_____

_____

_____

_____

_____

_____

_____

_____

_____

_____

_____

_____

_____

_____

# SELF-CARE CHECKLIST

*Check the ways you've taken care of*
*(or intend to take care of) yourself today:*

## REST DEEPLY

○ Prioritize nighttime sleep

○ Nap when the baby naps at least once a day

## EAT MINDFULLY

○ Nourish yourself with healthy meals and snacks

○ Drink plenty of water

## HONOR RELATIONSHIPS

○ Connect with your partner, a close friend, or a relative

○ Text or call a friend

## MOVE YOUR BEAUTIFUL BODY

○ Stretch in bed

○ Practice gentle yoga or Pilates

## BE KIND TO YOURSELF

○ Shower and brush teeth and hair

○ Open a window, breathe in fresh air, and smile

○ Practice meditation or breathwork

○ Pray, sing, or dance

○ Other: _____

## FEEL YOUR FEELINGS

○ Today I feel _____

## ASK FOR SUPPORT

*Today I could use help with . . .*

○ Holding the baby while I shower or rest

○ Preparing food

○ Laundry and cleaning

○ Other: _____

Today I will ask for help from _____

# DAY 11

Place your hands on your belly and womb area. Breathe deeply. What does your body feel like without a baby inside? What feelings are coming up for you?

_____

_____

_____

_____

_____

_____

_____

_____

_____

_____

_____

_____

_____

_____

_____

_____

_____

_____

_____

_____

# SELF-CARE CHECKLIST

*Check the ways you've taken care of*
*(or intend to take care of) yourself today:*

## REST DEEPLY

○ Prioritize nighttime sleep

○ Nap when the baby naps at least once a day

## EAT MINDFULLY

○ Nourish yourself with healthy meals and snacks

○ Drink plenty of water

## HONOR RELATIONSHIPS

○ Connect with your partner, a close friend, or a relative

○ Text or call a friend

## MOVE YOUR BEAUTIFUL BODY

○ Stretch in bed

○ Practice gentle yoga or Pilates

## BE KIND TO YOURSELF

○ Shower and brush teeth and hair

○ Open a window, breathe in fresh air, and smile

○ Practice meditation or breathwork

○ Pray, sing, or dance

○ Other: _____

## FEEL YOUR FEELINGS

○ Today I feel _____

## ASK FOR SUPPORT

*Today I could use help with . . .*

○ Holding the baby while I shower or rest

○ Preparing food

○ Laundry and cleaning

○ Other: _____

Today I will ask for help from _____

# DAY 12

It's common to worry about hurting your baby. What scary or uncomfortable thoughts are you having? *(If they feel overwhelming, debilitating, or intrusive, please reach out to a mental health professional for support.)*

_____

_____

_____

_____

_____

_____

_____

_____

_____

_____

_____

_____

_____

_____

_____

_____

_____

# SELF-CARE CHECKLIST

*Check the ways you've taken care of*
*(or intend to take care of) yourself today:*

## REST DEEPLY

○ Prioritize nighttime sleep

○ Nap when the baby naps at least once a day

## EAT MINDFULLY

○ Nourish yourself with healthy meals and snacks

○ Drink plenty of water

## HONOR RELATIONSHIPS

○ Connect with your partner, a close friend, or a relative

○ Text or call a friend

## MOVE YOUR BEAUTIFUL BODY

○ Stretch in bed

○ Practice gentle yoga or Pilates

## BE KIND TO YOURSELF

○ Shower and brush teeth and hair

○ Open a window, breathe in fresh air, and smile

○ Practice meditation or breathwork

○ Pray, sing, or dance

○ Other: _____

## FEEL YOUR FEELINGS

○ Today I feel _____

## ASK FOR SUPPORT

*Today I could use help with . . .*

○ Holding the baby while I shower or rest

○ Preparing food

○ Laundry and cleaning

○ Other: _____

Today I will ask for help from _____

# DAY 13

Slow down. Today's to-do list will be there again tomorrow. What are three things you can let go of until then so that today you can do less and be more present?

1. _____
_____
_____
_____
_____

2. _____
_____
_____
_____
_____

3. _____
_____
_____
_____
_____

# SELF-CARE CHECKLIST

*Check the ways you've taken care of
(or intend to take care of) yourself today:*

## REST DEEPLY

○ Prioritize nighttime sleep

○ Nap when the baby naps at least once a day

## EAT MINDFULLY

○ Nourish yourself with healthy meals and snacks

○ Drink plenty of water

## HONOR RELATIONSHIPS

○ Connect with your partner, a close friend, or a relative

○ Text or call a friend

## MOVE YOUR BEAUTIFUL BODY

○ Stretch in bed

○ Practice gentle yoga or Pilates

## BE KIND TO YOURSELF

○ Shower and brush teeth and hair

○ Open a window, breathe in fresh air, and smile

○ Practice meditation or breathwork

○ Pray, sing, or dance

○ Other: _____

## FEEL YOUR FEELINGS

○ Today I feel _____

## ASK FOR SUPPORT

*Today I could use help with . . .*

○ Holding the baby while I shower or rest

○ Preparing food

○ Laundry and cleaning

○ Other: _____

Today I will ask for help from _____

# DAY 14

What's something magical you experienced this week? Can you recall it in your mind? Now feel it in your heart ... and let it flow through your entire body. Describe the event and how you feel.

# SELF-CARE CHECKLIST

*Check the ways you've taken care of*
*(or intend to take care of) yourself today:*

## REST DEEPLY

○ Prioritize nighttime sleep

○ Nap when the baby naps at least once a day

## EAT MINDFULLY

○ Nourish yourself with healthy meals and snacks

○ Drink plenty of water

## HONOR RELATIONSHIPS

○ Connect with your partner, a close friend, or a relative

○ Text or call a friend

## MOVE YOUR BEAUTIFUL BODY

○ Stretch in bed

○ Practice gentle yoga or Pilates

## BE KIND TO YOURSELF

○ Shower and brush teeth and hair

○ Open a window, breathe in fresh air, and smile

○ Practice meditation or breathwork

○ Pray, sing, or dance

○ Other: _____

## FEEL YOUR FEELINGS

○ Today I feel _____

## ASK FOR SUPPORT

*Today I could use help with . . .*

○ Holding the baby while I shower or rest

○ Preparing food

○ Laundry and cleaning

○ Other: _____

Today I will ask for help from _____

# DAY 15

Move your body oh so gently. To prevent prolapse and encourage recovery, lie down often and exercise gently. What are three ways you can move your body with little to no stress on your pelvic floor? *(Think stretching, postnatal yoga, or Pilates for now, and wait on the running, jumping, and ab work.)*

1. _____

   _____

   _____

   _____

   _____

2. _____

   _____

   _____

   _____

   _____

3. _____

   _____

   _____

   _____

   _____

# SELF-CARE CHECKLIST

*Check the ways you've taken care of*
*(or intend to take care of) yourself today:*

## REST DEEPLY

○ Prioritize nighttime sleep

○ Nap when the baby naps at least once a day

## EAT MINDFULLY

○ Nourish yourself with healthy meals and snacks

○ Drink plenty of water

## HONOR RELATIONSHIPS

○ Connect with your partner, a close friend, or a relative

○ Text or call a friend

## MOVE YOUR BEAUTIFUL BODY

○ Stretch in bed

○ Practice gentle yoga or Pilates

## BE KIND TO YOURSELF

○ Shower and brush teeth and hair

○ Open a window, breathe in fresh air, and smile

○ Practice meditation or breathwork

○ Pray, sing, or dance

○ Other: _____

## FEEL YOUR FEELINGS

○ Today I feel _____

## ASK FOR SUPPORT

*Today I could use help with . . .*

○ Holding the baby while I shower or rest

○ Preparing food

○ Laundry and cleaning

○ Other: _____

Today I will ask for help from _____

# DAY 16

Practice being kind to yourself. Choose a mantra such as "It's okay to make mistakes" or "Motherhood is hard, and I'm learning as I go," or craft your own. Write down your mama mantra five times.

1. _____
_____
_____

2. _____
_____
_____

3. _____
_____
_____

4. _____
_____
_____

5. _____
_____
_____

# SELF-CARE CHECKLIST

*Check the ways you've taken care of*
*(or intend to take care of) yourself today:*

## REST DEEPLY

○ Prioritize nighttime sleep

○ Nap when the baby naps at least once a day

## EAT MINDFULLY

○ Nourish yourself with healthy meals and snacks

○ Drink plenty of water

## HONOR RELATIONSHIPS

○ Connect with your partner, a close friend, or a relative

○ Text or call a friend

## MOVE YOUR BEAUTIFUL BODY

○ Stretch in bed

○ Practice gentle yoga or Pilates

## BE KIND TO YOURSELF

○ Shower and brush teeth and hair

○ Open a window, breathe in fresh air, and smile

○ Practice meditation or breathwork

○ Pray, sing, or dance

○ Other: _____

## FEEL YOUR FEELINGS

○ Today I feel _____

## ASK FOR SUPPORT

*Today I could use help with . . .*

○ Holding the baby while I shower or rest

○ Preparing food

○ Laundry and cleaning

○ Other: _____

Today I will ask for help from _____

# DAY 17

Self-care isn't a luxury—it's a necessity. What do you want self-care to look like for you these days? What is one kind thing you can do for yourself today to move in that direction?

_____

_____

_____

_____

_____

_____

_____

_____

_____

_____

_____

_____

_____

_____

_____

_____

_____

_____

_____

_____

# SELF-CARE CHECKLIST

*Check the ways you've taken care of*
*(or intend to take care of) yourself today:*

## REST DEEPLY

○ Prioritize nighttime sleep

○ Nap when the baby naps at least once a day

## EAT MINDFULLY

○ Nourish yourself with healthy meals and snacks

○ Drink plenty of water

## HONOR RELATIONSHIPS

○ Connect with your partner, a close friend, or a relative

○ Text or call a friend

## MOVE YOUR BEAUTIFUL BODY

○ Stretch in bed

○ Practice gentle yoga or Pilates

## BE KIND TO YOURSELF

○ Shower and brush teeth and hair

○ Open a window, breathe in fresh air, and smile

○ Practice meditation or breathwork

○ Pray, sing, or dance

○ Other: _____

## FEEL YOUR FEELINGS

○ Today I feel _____

## ASK FOR SUPPORT

*Today I could use help with . . .*

○ Holding the baby while I shower or rest

○ Preparing food

○ Laundry and cleaning

○ Other: _____

Today I will ask for help from _____

# DAY 18

Honor your body for creating, making, and birthing a baby.
Write out five thank-you affirmations to the parts of your body
you're feeling grateful for *("Thank you, womb, for . . . ," "Thank you,*
*heart, for . . . ," etc.).*

1. _____

_____

_____

2. _____

_____

_____

3. _____

_____

_____

4. _____

_____

_____

5. _____

_____

_____

# SELF-CARE CHECKLIST

*Check the ways you've taken care of*
*(or intend to take care of) yourself today:*

## REST DEEPLY

○ Prioritize nighttime sleep

○ Nap when the baby naps at least once a day

## EAT MINDFULLY

○ Nourish yourself with healthy meals and snacks

○ Drink plenty of water

## HONOR RELATIONSHIPS

○ Connect with your partner, a close friend, or a relative

○ Text or call a friend

## MOVE YOUR BEAUTIFUL BODY

○ Stretch in bed

○ Practice gentle yoga or Pilates

## BE KIND TO YOURSELF

○ Shower and brush teeth and hair

○ Open a window, breathe in fresh air, and smile

○ Practice meditation or breathwork

○ Pray, sing, or dance

○ Other: _____

## FEEL YOUR FEELINGS

○ Today I feel _____

## ASK FOR SUPPORT

*Today I could use help with . . .*

○ Holding the baby while I shower or rest

○ Preparing food

○ Laundry and cleaning

○ Other: _____

Today I will ask for help from _____

# DAY 19

Prioritize yourself. The next time you have 30 minutes of alone time, maybe while babe naps, what will you do? *(Yoga? Sit alone in stillness? Call a friend? Read?)*

_____

_____

_____

_____

_____

_____

_____

_____

_____

_____

_____

_____

_____

_____

_____

_____

_____

_____

# SELF-CARE CHECKLIST

*Check the ways you've taken care of*
*(or intend to take care of) yourself today:*

## REST DEEPLY

- ○ Prioritize nighttime sleep
- ○ Nap when the baby naps at least once a day

## EAT MINDFULLY

- ○ Nourish yourself with healthy meals and snacks
- ○ Drink plenty of water

## HONOR RELATIONSHIPS

- ○ Connect with your partner, a close friend, or a relative
- ○ Text or call a friend

## MOVE YOUR BEAUTIFUL BODY

- ○ Stretch in bed
- ○ Practice gentle yoga or Pilates

## BE KIND TO YOURSELF

- ○ Shower and brush teeth and hair
- ○ Practice meditation or breathwork
- ○ Open a window, breathe in fresh air, and smile
- ○ Pray, sing, or dance
- ○ Other: _____

## FEEL YOUR FEELINGS

- ○ Today I feel _____

## ASK FOR SUPPORT

*Today I could use help with . . .*

- ○ Holding the baby while I shower or rest
- ○ Laundry and cleaning
- ○ Other: _____
- ○ Preparing food

Today I will ask for help from _____

# DAY 20

Cherish your connections. List the three most important people in your life right now and what you love about them.

**1.** _____

_____

_____

_____

_____

**2.** _____

_____

_____

_____

_____

**3.** _____

_____

_____

_____

_____

# SELF-CARE CHECKLIST

*Check the ways you've taken care of*
*(or intend to take care of) yourself today:*

## REST DEEPLY

○ Prioritize nighttime sleep

○ Nap when the baby naps at least once a day

## EAT MINDFULLY

○ Nourish yourself with healthy meals and snacks

○ Drink plenty of water

## HONOR RELATIONSHIPS

○ Connect with your partner, a close friend, or a relative

○ Text or call a friend

## MOVE YOUR BEAUTIFUL BODY

○ Stretch in bed

○ Practice gentle yoga or Pilates

## BE KIND TO YOURSELF

○ Shower and brush teeth and hair

○ Open a window, breathe in fresh air, and smile

○ Practice meditation or breathwork

○ Pray, sing, or dance

○ Other: _____

## FEEL YOUR FEELINGS

○ Today I feel _____

## ASK FOR SUPPORT

*Today I could use help with . . .*

○ Holding the baby while I shower or rest

○ Preparing food

○ Laundry and cleaning

○ Other: _____

Today I will ask for help from _____

# DAY 21

Interrupted sleep, your newborn crying, and scrambling to learn how to parent can put an enormous amount of stress on your body. Take time to rest as deeply and as often as you can. List three ways you can let yourself rest, and choose one to practice today *(yoga nidra, take a nap, etc.).*

1. _____

_____

_____

_____

2. _____

_____

_____

_____

3. _____

_____

_____

_____

# SELF-CARE CHECKLIST

*Check the ways you've taken care of
(or intend to take care of) yourself today:*

## REST DEEPLY

○ Prioritize nighttime sleep

○ Nap when the baby naps at
least once a day

## EAT MINDFULLY

○ Nourish yourself with
healthy meals and snacks

○ Drink plenty of water

## HONOR RELATIONSHIPS

○ Connect with your partner,
a close friend, or a relative

○ Text or call a friend

## MOVE YOUR BEAUTIFUL BODY

○ Stretch in bed

○ Practice gentle
yoga or Pilates

## BE KIND TO YOURSELF

○ Shower and brush
teeth and hair

○ Open a window, breathe in
fresh air, and smile

○ Practice meditation
or breathwork

○ Pray, sing, or dance

○ Other: _____

## FEEL YOUR FEELINGS

○ Today I feel _____

## ASK FOR SUPPORT

*Today I could use help with . . .*

○ Holding the baby while I
shower or rest

○ Preparing food

○ Laundry and cleaning

○ Other: _____

Today I will ask for help from _____

# DAY 22

How did you access and express your creative energy before
having a baby? How can you incorporate these practices into
your life today, even in a small way?

_____

_____

_____

_____

_____

_____

_____

_____

_____

_____

_____

_____

_____

_____

_____

_____

_____

_____

# SELF-CARE CHECKLIST

*Check the ways you've taken care of*
*(or intend to take care of) yourself today:*

## REST DEEPLY

○ Prioritize nighttime sleep

○ Nap when the baby naps at least once a day

## EAT MINDFULLY

○ Nourish yourself with healthy meals and snacks

○ Drink plenty of water

## HONOR RELATIONSHIPS

○ Connect with your partner, a close friend, or a relative

○ Text or call a friend

## MOVE YOUR BEAUTIFUL BODY

○ Stretch in bed

○ Practice gentle yoga or Pilates

## BE KIND TO YOURSELF

○ Shower and brush teeth and hair

○ Open a window, breathe in fresh air, and smile

○ Practice meditation or breathwork

○ Pray, sing, or dance

○ Other: _____

## FEEL YOUR FEELINGS

○ Today I feel _____

## ASK FOR SUPPORT

*Today I could use help with . . .*

○ Holding the baby while I shower or rest

○ Preparing food

○ Laundry and cleaning

○ Other: _____

Today I will ask for help from _____

# DAY 23

List five ways your body amazes you *(knows how to make a baby, heal and recover, etc.)*.

1. _____
   _____
   _____

2. _____
   _____
   _____

3. _____
   _____
   _____

4. _____
   _____
   _____

5. _____
   _____
   _____

# SELF-CARE CHECKLIST

*Check the ways you've taken care of
(or intend to take care of) yourself today:*

## REST DEEPLY

○ Prioritize nighttime sleep

○ Nap when the baby naps at least once a day

## EAT MINDFULLY

○ Nourish yourself with healthy meals and snacks

○ Drink plenty of water

## HONOR RELATIONSHIPS

○ Connect with your partner, a close friend, or a relative

○ Text or call a friend

## MOVE YOUR BEAUTIFUL BODY

○ Stretch in bed

○ Practice gentle yoga or Pilates

## BE KIND TO YOURSELF

○ Shower and brush teeth and hair

○ Open a window, breathe in fresh air, and smile

○ Practice meditation or breathwork

○ Pray, sing, or dance

○ Other: _____

## FEEL YOUR FEELINGS

○ Today I feel _____

## ASK FOR SUPPORT

*Today I could use help with . . .*

○ Holding the baby while I shower or rest

○ Preparing food

○ Laundry and cleaning

○ Other: _____

Today I will ask for help from _____

# DAY 24

The to-do list never ends. Take a moment to add yourself to the list. *(Psst, don't put yourself at the bottom of the list, okay?)* Check in and ask: What do I need today?

_____

_____

_____

_____

_____

_____

_____

_____

_____

_____

_____

_____

_____

_____

_____

_____

_____

_____

_____

_____

_____

# SELF-CARE CHECKLIST

*Check the ways you've taken care of*
*(or intend to take care of) yourself today:*

## REST DEEPLY

○ Prioritize nighttime sleep

○ Nap when the baby naps at least once a day

## EAT MINDFULLY

○ Nourish yourself with healthy meals and snacks

○ Drink plenty of water

## HONOR RELATIONSHIPS

○ Connect with your partner, a close friend, or a relative

○ Text or call a friend

## MOVE YOUR BEAUTIFUL BODY

○ Stretch in bed

○ Practice gentle yoga or Pilates

## BE KIND TO YOURSELF

○ Shower and brush teeth and hair

○ Open a window, breathe in fresh air, and smile

○ Practice meditation or breathwork

○ Pray, sing, or dance

○ Other: _____

## FEEL YOUR FEELINGS

○ Today I feel _____

## ASK FOR SUPPORT

*Today I could use help with . . .*

○ Holding the baby while I shower or rest

○ Preparing food

○ Laundry and cleaning

○ Other: _____

Today I will ask for help from _____

# DAY 25

What are you passionate about? List all of the activities, ideas, hobbies, and causes that are near and dear to your heart. *(Book-mark this page and reread this list to stay connected to your passions when motherhood feels all-consuming.)*

# SELF-CARE CHECKLIST

*Check the ways you've taken care of
(or intend to take care of) yourself today:*

## REST DEEPLY

○ Prioritize nighttime sleep

○ Nap when the baby naps at least once a day

## EAT MINDFULLY

○ Nourish yourself with healthy meals and snacks

○ Drink plenty of water

## HONOR RELATIONSHIPS

○ Connect with your partner, a close friend, or a relative

○ Text or call a friend

## MOVE YOUR BEAUTIFUL BODY

○ Stretch in bed

○ Practice gentle yoga or Pilates

## BE KIND TO YOURSELF

○ Shower and brush teeth and hair

○ Open a window, breathe in fresh air, and smile

○ Practice meditation or breathwork

○ Pray, sing, or dance

○ Other: _____

## FEEL YOUR FEELINGS

○ Today I feel _____

## ASK FOR SUPPORT

*Today I could use help with . . .*

○ Holding the baby while I shower or rest

○ Preparing food

○ Laundry and cleaning

○ Other: _____

Today I will ask for help from _____

# DAY 26

Your body is full of wisdom. Take a moment to listen with loving-kindness to your belly. If your belly could talk, what would it say to you?

_____

_____

_____

_____

_____

_____

_____

_____

_____

_____

_____

_____

_____

_____

_____

_____

_____

_____

_____

# SELF-CARE CHECKLIST

*Check the ways you've taken care of
(or intend to take care of) yourself today:*

## REST DEEPLY

○ Prioritize nighttime sleep

○ Nap when the baby naps at least once a day

## EAT MINDFULLY

○ Nourish yourself with healthy meals and snacks

○ Drink plenty of water

## HONOR RELATIONSHIPS

○ Connect with your partner, a close friend, or a relative

○ Text or call a friend

## MOVE YOUR BEAUTIFUL BODY

○ Stretch in bed

○ Practice gentle yoga or Pilates

## BE KIND TO YOURSELF

○ Shower and brush teeth and hair

○ Open a window, breathe in fresh air, and smile

○ Practice meditation or breathwork

○ Pray, sing, or dance

○ Other: _____

## FEEL YOUR FEELINGS

○ Today I feel _____

## ASK FOR SUPPORT

*Today I could use help with . . .*

○ Holding the baby while I shower or rest

○ Preparing food

○ Laundry and cleaning

○ Other: _____

Today I will ask for help from _____

# DAY 27

What are your favorite ways to connect with your favorite person *(partner, close friend, or family member)*? How does it look different to connect in this way with your baby in your life?

_____

_____

_____

_____

_____

_____

_____

_____

_____

_____

_____

_____

_____

_____

_____

_____

_____

_____

_____

# SELF-CARE CHECKLIST

*Check the ways you've taken care of
(or intend to take care of) yourself today:*

## REST DEEPLY

○ Prioritize nighttime sleep

○ Nap when the baby naps at least once a day

## EAT MINDFULLY

○ Nourish yourself with healthy meals and snacks

○ Drink plenty of water

## HONOR RELATIONSHIPS

○ Connect with your partner, a close friend, or a relative

○ Text or call a friend

## MOVE YOUR BEAUTIFUL BODY

○ Stretch in bed

○ Practice gentle yoga or Pilates

## BE KIND TO YOURSELF

○ Shower and brush teeth and hair

○ Open a window, breathe in fresh air, and smile

○ Practice meditation or breathwork

○ Pray, sing, or dance

○ Other: _____

## FEEL YOUR FEELINGS

○ Today I feel _____

## ASK FOR SUPPORT

*Today I could use help with . . .*

○ Holding the baby while I shower or rest

○ Preparing food

○ Laundry and cleaning

○ Other: _____

Today I will ask for help from _____

# DAY 28

You grew your baby, birthed your baby, and now feed and nourish your baby. How has breastfeeding or bottle-feeding your babe been emotionally, physically, and spiritually?

_____

_____

_____

_____

_____

_____

_____

_____

_____

_____

_____

_____

_____

_____

_____

_____

_____

_____

# SELF-CARE CHECKLIST

*Check the ways you've taken care of
(or intend to take care of) yourself today:*

## REST DEEPLY

○ Prioritize nighttime sleep

○ Nap when the baby naps at least once a day

## EAT MINDFULLY

○ Nourish yourself with healthy meals and snacks

○ Drink plenty of water

## HONOR RELATIONSHIPS

○ Connect with your partner, a close friend, or a relative

○ Text or call a friend

## MOVE YOUR BEAUTIFUL BODY

○ Stretch in bed

○ Practice gentle yoga or Pilates

## BE KIND TO YOURSELF

○ Shower and brush teeth and hair

○ Open a window, breathe in fresh air, and smile

○ Practice meditation or breathwork

○ Pray, sing, or dance

○ Other: _____

## FEEL YOUR FEELINGS

○ Today I feel _____

## ASK FOR SUPPORT

*Today I could use help with . . .*

○ Holding the baby while I shower or rest

○ Preparing food

○ Laundry and cleaning

○ Other: _____

Today I will ask for help from _____

# DAY 29

Stay inspired. Make a list of your "happy places," all the inspiring and gorgeous places in the world you've visited or dreamed of visiting, and what you love about them.

# SELF-CARE CHECKLIST

*Check the ways you've taken care of
(or intend to take care of) yourself today:*

## REST DEEPLY

○ Prioritize nighttime sleep

○ Nap when the baby naps at least once a day

## EAT MINDFULLY

○ Nourish yourself with healthy meals and snacks

○ Drink plenty of water

## HONOR RELATIONSHIPS

○ Connect with your partner, a close friend, or a relative

○ Text or call a friend

## MOVE YOUR BEAUTIFUL BODY

○ Stretch in bed

○ Practice gentle yoga or Pilates

## BE KIND TO YOURSELF

○ Shower and brush teeth and hair

○ Open a window, breathe in fresh air, and smile

○ Practice meditation or breathwork

○ Pray, sing, or dance

○ Other: _____

## FEEL YOUR FEELINGS

○ Today I feel _____

## ASK FOR SUPPORT

*Today I could use help with . . .*

○ Holding the baby while I shower or rest

○ Preparing food

○ Laundry and cleaning

○ Other: _____

Today I will ask for help from _____

# DAY 30

Find your feet. Wiggle your toes. Press your feet and legs deeply into the ground. What does being present and physically grounded mean to you? How does it feel?

# SELF-CARE CHECKLIST

*Check the ways you've taken care of
(or intend to take care of) yourself today:*

## REST DEEPLY

○ Prioritize nighttime sleep

○ Nap when the baby naps at least once a day

## EAT MINDFULLY

○ Nourish yourself with healthy meals and snacks

○ Drink plenty of water

## HONOR RELATIONSHIPS

○ Connect with your partner, a close friend, or a relative

○ Text or call a friend

## MOVE YOUR BEAUTIFUL BODY

○ Stretch in bed

○ Practice gentle yoga or Pilates

## BE KIND TO YOURSELF

○ Shower and brush teeth and hair

○ Open a window, breathe in fresh air, and smile

○ Practice meditation or breathwork

○ Pray, sing, or dance

○ Other: _____

## FEEL YOUR FEELINGS

○ Today I feel _____

## ASK FOR SUPPORT

*Today I could use help with . . .*

○ Holding the baby while I shower or rest

○ Preparing food

○ Laundry and cleaning

○ Other: _____

Today I will ask for help from _____

# DAY 31

Think about your physical, mental, emotional, and spiritual well-being. List five things you could use support with right now *(anxiety symptoms, healthy eating, managing physical pain, etc.)* and who you could ask for help *(therapist, food delivery, chiropractor, etc.)*.

1. _____

_____

_____

2. _____

_____

_____

3. _____

_____

_____

4. _____

_____

_____

5. _____

_____

_____

# SELF-CARE CHECKLIST

*Check the ways you've taken care of*
*(or intend to take care of) yourself today:*

## REST DEEPLY

○ Prioritize nighttime sleep

○ Nap when the baby naps at least once a day

## EAT MINDFULLY

○ Nourish yourself with healthy meals and snacks

○ Drink plenty of water

## HONOR RELATIONSHIPS

○ Connect with your partner, a close friend, or a relative

○ Text or call a friend

## MOVE YOUR BEAUTIFUL BODY

○ Stretch in bed

○ Practice gentle yoga or Pilates

## BE KIND TO YOURSELF

○ Shower and brush teeth and hair

○ Open a window, breathe in fresh air, and smile

○ Practice meditation or breathwork

○ Pray, sing, or dance

○ Other: _____

## FEEL YOUR FEELINGS

○ Today I feel _____

## ASK FOR SUPPORT

*Today I could use help with . . .*

○ Holding the baby while I shower or rest

○ Preparing food

○ Laundry and cleaning

○ Other: _____

Today I will ask for help from _____

# DAY 32

Your sexual exergy is nourishing, life-force energy. It's easy to lose touch with this part of yourself in early motherhood. List three ways you can connect with your sensuality.

1. _____

_____

_____

_____

_____

2. _____

_____

_____

_____

_____

3. _____

_____

_____

_____

_____

# SELF-CARE CHECKLIST

*Check the ways you've taken care of*
*(or intend to take care of) yourself today:*

## REST DEEPLY

○ Prioritize nighttime sleep

○ Nap when the baby naps at least once a day

## EAT MINDFULLY

○ Nourish yourself with healthy meals and snacks

○ Drink plenty of water

## HONOR RELATIONSHIPS

○ Connect with your partner, a close friend, or a relative

○ Text or call a friend

## MOVE YOUR BEAUTIFUL BODY

○ Stretch in bed

○ Practice gentle yoga or Pilates

## BE KIND TO YOURSELF

○ Shower and brush teeth and hair

○ Open a window, breathe in fresh air, and smile

○ Practice meditation or breathwork

○ Pray, sing, or dance

○ Other: _____

## FEEL YOUR FEELINGS

○ Today I feel _____

## ASK FOR SUPPORT

*Today I could use help with . . .*

○ Holding the baby while I shower or rest

○ Preparing food

○ Laundry and cleaning

○ Other: _____

Today I will ask for help from _____

# DAY 33

It's common to have bladder issues, prolapse, or abdominal separation. Getting help for healing now, not later, is critical. Do you have any uncomfortable or concerning symptoms or changes in your body? Who can you call for help?

# SELF-CARE CHECKLIST

*Check the ways you've taken care of*
*(or intend to take care of) yourself today:*

## REST DEEPLY

○ Prioritize nighttime sleep

○ Nap when the baby naps at least once a day

## EAT MINDFULLY

○ Nourish yourself with healthy meals and snacks

○ Drink plenty of water

## HONOR RELATIONSHIPS

○ Connect with your partner, a close friend, or a relative

○ Text or call a friend

## MOVE YOUR BEAUTIFUL BODY

○ Stretch in bed

○ Practice gentle yoga or Pilates

## BE KIND TO YOURSELF

○ Shower and brush teeth and hair

○ Open a window, breathe in fresh air, and smile

○ Practice meditation or breathwork

○ Pray, sing, or dance

○ Other: _____

## FEEL YOUR FEELINGS

○ Today I feel _____

## ASK FOR SUPPORT

*Today I could use help with . . .*

○ Holding the baby while I shower or rest

○ Preparing food

○ Laundry and cleaning

○ Other: _____

Today I will ask for help from _____

# DAY 34

Learning to trust your intuition *(aka your mama gut)* takes practice.
Breathe deeply to slow your thoughts, and then check in with
your heart space. What is your heart whispering today?

_____

_____

_____

_____

_____

_____

_____

_____

_____

_____

_____

_____

_____

_____

_____

_____

_____

_____

_____

_____

_____

# SELF-CARE CHECKLIST

*Check the ways you've taken care of*
*(or intend to take care of) yourself today:*

## REST DEEPLY

○ Prioritize nighttime sleep

○ Nap when the baby naps at least once a day

## EAT MINDFULLY

○ Nourish yourself with healthy meals and snacks

○ Drink plenty of water

## HONOR RELATIONSHIPS

○ Connect with your partner, a close friend, or a relative

○ Text or call a friend

## MOVE YOUR BEAUTIFUL BODY

○ Stretch in bed

○ Practice gentle yoga or Pilates

## BE KIND TO YOURSELF

○ Shower and brush teeth and hair

○ Open a window, breathe in fresh air, and smile

○ Practice meditation or breathwork

○ Pray, sing, or dance

○ Other: _____

## FEEL YOUR FEELINGS

○ Today I feel _____

## ASK FOR SUPPORT

*Today I could use help with . . .*

○ Holding the baby while I shower or rest

○ Preparing food

○ Laundry and cleaning

○ Other: _____

Today I will ask for help from _____

# DAY 35

You are a strong, resilient human. List two of the hardest things you've experienced in your life and what you've learned from each experience.

1. _____
_____
_____
_____
_____
_____
_____
_____
_____
_____

2. _____
_____
_____
_____
_____
_____
_____
_____
_____
_____

# SELF-CARE CHECKLIST

*Check the ways you've taken care of*
*(or intend to take care of) yourself today:*

## REST DEEPLY

○ Prioritize nighttime sleep

○ Nap when the baby naps at least once a day

## EAT MINDFULLY

○ Nourish yourself with healthy meals and snacks

○ Drink plenty of water

## HONOR RELATIONSHIPS

○ Connect with your partner, a close friend, or a relative

○ Text or call a friend

## MOVE YOUR BEAUTIFUL BODY

○ Stretch in bed

○ Practice gentle yoga or Pilates

## BE KIND TO YOURSELF

○ Shower and brush teeth and hair

○ Open a window, breathe in fresh air, and smile

○ Practice meditation or breathwork

○ Pray, sing, or dance

○ Other: _____

## FEEL YOUR FEELINGS

○ Today I feel _____

## ASK FOR SUPPORT

*Today I could use help with . . .*

○ Holding the baby while I shower or rest

○ Preparing food

○ Laundry and cleaning

○ Other: _____

Today I will ask for help from _____

# DAY 36

Stop and drop. Sometimes the most nourishing thing you can do is lie down and stop moving. What is your body asking of you? What does it need today?

_____

_____

_____

_____

_____

_____

_____

_____

_____

_____

_____

_____

_____

_____

_____

_____

_____

_____

_____

_____

# SELF-CARE CHECKLIST

*Check the ways you've taken care of*
*(or intend to take care of) yourself today:*

## REST DEEPLY

○ Prioritize nighttime sleep

○ Nap when the baby naps at least once a day

## EAT MINDFULLY

○ Nourish yourself with healthy meals and snacks

○ Drink plenty of water

## HONOR RELATIONSHIPS

○ Connect with your partner, a close friend, or a relative

○ Text or call a friend

## MOVE YOUR BEAUTIFUL BODY

○ Stretch in bed

○ Practice gentle yoga or Pilates

## BE KIND TO YOURSELF

○ Shower and brush teeth and hair

○ Open a window, breathe in fresh air, and smile

○ Practice meditation or breathwork

○ Pray, sing, or dance

○ Other: _____

## FEEL YOUR FEELINGS

○ Today I feel _____

## ASK FOR SUPPORT

*Today I could use help with . . .*

○ Holding the baby while I shower or rest

○ Preparing food

○ Laundry and cleaning

○ Other: _____

Today I will ask for help from _____

# DAY 37

Welcome all the feelings. And I mean *all* the feelings. Finish this thought:

**Today I am feeling** _____

_____

_____

_____

_____

_____

_____

_____

_____

_____

_____

_____

_____

_____

_____

_____

_____

_____

_____

# SELF-CARE CHECKLIST

*Check the ways you've taken care of*
*(or intend to take care of) yourself today:*

## REST DEEPLY

○ Prioritize nighttime sleep

○ Nap when the baby naps at least once a day

## EAT MINDFULLY

○ Nourish yourself with healthy meals and snacks

○ Drink plenty of water

## HONOR RELATIONSHIPS

○ Connect with your partner, a close friend, or a relative

○ Text or call a friend

## MOVE YOUR BEAUTIFUL BODY

○ Stretch in bed

○ Practice gentle yoga or Pilates

## BE KIND TO YOURSELF

○ Shower and brush teeth and hair

○ Open a window, breathe in fresh air, and smile

○ Practice meditation or breathwork

○ Pray, sing, or dance

○ Other: _____

## FEEL YOUR FEELINGS

○ Today I feel _____

## ASK FOR SUPPORT

*Today I could use help with . . .*

○ Holding the baby while I shower or rest

○ Preparing food

○ Laundry and cleaning

○ Other: _____

Today I will ask for help from _____

# DAY 38

Honor the sacred. Write down all the practices that help you connect to your highest self and source *(meditation, yoga, music, dancing, reading, journaling, painting, listening to inspirational podcasts, etc.).*

# SELF-CARE CHECKLIST

*Check the ways you've taken care of
(or intend to take care of) yourself today:*

## REST DEEPLY

○ Prioritize nighttime sleep

○ Nap when the baby naps at least once a day

## EAT MINDFULLY

○ Nourish yourself with healthy meals and snacks

○ Drink plenty of water

## HONOR RELATIONSHIPS

○ Connect with your partner, a close friend, or a relative

○ Text or call a friend

## MOVE YOUR BEAUTIFUL BODY

○ Stretch in bed

○ Practice gentle yoga or Pilates

## BE KIND TO YOURSELF

○ Shower and brush teeth and hair

○ Open a window, breathe in fresh air, and smile

○ Practice meditation or breathwork

○ Pray, sing, or dance

○ Other: _____

## FEEL YOUR FEELINGS

○ Today I feel _____

## ASK FOR SUPPORT

*Today I could use help with . . .*

○ Holding the baby while I shower or rest

○ Preparing food

○ Laundry and cleaning

○ Other: _____

Today I will ask for help from _____

# DAY 39

Motherhood has a steep learning curve. It's completely normal to feel lost and have no idea what you're doing. What's your biggest worry right now? What person or resource can you turn to for help?

_____

_____

_____

_____

_____

_____

_____

_____

_____

_____

_____

_____

_____

_____

_____

_____

_____

# SELF-CARE CHECKLIST

*Check the ways you've taken care of*
*(or intend to take care of) yourself today:*

## REST DEEPLY

○ Prioritize nighttime sleep

○ Nap when the baby naps at least once a day

## EAT MINDFULLY

○ Nourish yourself with healthy meals and snacks

○ Drink plenty of water

## HONOR RELATIONSHIPS

○ Connect with your partner, a close friend, or a relative

○ Text or call a friend

## MOVE YOUR BEAUTIFUL BODY

○ Stretch in bed

○ Practice gentle yoga or Pilates

## BE KIND TO YOURSELF

○ Shower and brush teeth and hair

○ Open a window, breathe in fresh air, and smile

○ Practice meditation or breathwork

○ Pray, sing, or dance

○ Other: _____

## FEEL YOUR FEELINGS

○ Today I feel _____

## ASK FOR SUPPORT

*Today I could use help with . . .*

○ Holding the baby while I shower or rest

○ Preparing food

○ Laundry and cleaning

○ Other: _____

Today I will ask for help from _____

# DAY 40

Laughter is an epic stress reliever. Find ways to laugh often. Make a list of five things you can do to laugh when you feel stressed *(watch memes or a comedy show, etc.)*.

1. _____

_____

_____

2. _____

_____

_____

3. _____

_____

_____

4. _____

_____

_____

5. _____

_____

_____

# SELF-CARE CHECKLIST

*Check the ways you've taken care of*
*(or intend to take care of) yourself today:*

## REST DEEPLY

○ Prioritize nighttime sleep

○ Nap when the baby naps at least once a day

## EAT MINDFULLY

○ Nourish yourself with healthy meals and snacks

○ Drink plenty of water

## HONOR RELATIONSHIPS

○ Connect with your partner, a close friend, or a relative

○ Text or call a friend

## MOVE YOUR BEAUTIFUL BODY

○ Stretch in bed

○ Practice gentle yoga or Pilates

## BE KIND TO YOURSELF

○ Shower and brush teeth and hair

○ Practice meditation or breathwork

○ Open a window, breathe in fresh air, and smile

○ Pray, sing, or dance

○ Other: _____

## FEEL YOUR FEELINGS

○ Today I feel _____

## ASK FOR SUPPORT

*Today I could use help with . . .*

○ Holding the baby while I shower or rest

○ Laundry and cleaning

○ Other: _____

○ Preparing food

Today I will ask for help from _____

# DAY 41

Feelings come and go like waves. You can practice using your breath to support your emotions. What feelings do you want more of today? Breathe them in . . . What feelings do you want less of today? Let them go with each exhale . . .

**I inhale** *(patience, love, etc.)* _____

_____

_____

_____

_____

_____

_____

_____

**I exhale** *(fear, insecurity, etc.)* _____

_____

_____

_____

_____

_____

_____

_____

# SELF-CARE CHECKLIST

*Check the ways you've taken care of*
*(or intend to take care of) yourself today:*

## REST DEEPLY

○ Prioritize nighttime sleep

○ Nap when the baby naps at least once a day

## EAT MINDFULLY

○ Nourish yourself with healthy meals and snacks

○ Drink plenty of water

## HONOR RELATIONSHIPS

○ Connect with your partner, a close friend, or a relative

○ Text or call a friend

## MOVE YOUR BEAUTIFUL BODY

○ Stretch in bed

○ Practice gentle yoga or Pilates

## BE KIND TO YOURSELF

○ Shower and brush teeth and hair

○ Open a window, breathe in fresh air, and smile

○ Practice meditation or breathwork

○ Pray, sing, or dance

○ Other: _____

## FEEL YOUR FEELINGS

○ Today I feel _____

## ASK FOR SUPPORT

*Today I could use help with . . .*

○ Holding the baby while I shower or rest

○ Preparing food

○ Laundry and cleaning

○ Other: _____

Today I will ask for help from _____

# DAY 42

Postpartum isn't over after six weeks. Your recovery and postpartum journey is unique. What are three things that are surprising to you in your second month of motherhood?

1. _____

_____

_____

_____

_____

2. _____

_____

_____

_____

_____

3. _____

_____

_____

_____

_____

# SELF-CARE CHECKLIST

*Check the ways you've taken care of*
*(or intend to take care of) yourself today:*

## REST DEEPLY

○ Prioritize nighttime sleep

○ Nap when the baby naps at least once a day

## EAT MINDFULLY

○ Nourish yourself with healthy meals and snacks

○ Drink plenty of water

## HONOR RELATIONSHIPS

○ Connect with your partner, a close friend, or a relative

○ Text or call a friend

## MOVE YOUR BEAUTIFUL BODY

○ Stretch in bed

○ Practice gentle yoga or Pilates

## BE KIND TO YOURSELF

○ Shower and brush teeth and hair

○ Open a window, breathe in fresh air, and smile

○ Practice meditation or breathwork

○ Pray, sing, or dance

○ Other: _____

## FEEL YOUR FEELINGS

○ Today I feel _____

## ASK FOR SUPPORT

*Today I could use help with . . .*

○ Holding the baby while I shower or rest

○ Preparing food

○ Laundry and cleaning

○ Other: _____

Today I will ask for help from _____

# DAY 43

It's common to feel overstimulated or "touched out" from constant contact with your baby. To counter this, meaningful physical connection with your partner *(or a close friend)* can be deeply nourishing. What kind of physical contact would feel good right now? *(Think foot massage, a hug, holding hands, etc.)*

_____

_____

_____

_____

_____

_____

_____

_____

_____

_____

_____

_____

_____

_____

_____

_____

_____

_____

_____

# SELF-CARE CHECKLIST

*Check the ways you've taken care of*
*(or intend to take care of) yourself today:*

## REST DEEPLY

○ Prioritize nighttime sleep

○ Nap when the baby naps at least once a day

## EAT MINDFULLY

○ Nourish yourself with healthy meals and snacks

○ Drink plenty of water

## HONOR RELATIONSHIPS

○ Connect with your partner, a close friend, or a relative

○ Text or call a friend

## MOVE YOUR BEAUTIFUL BODY

○ Stretch in bed

○ Practice gentle yoga or Pilates

## BE KIND TO YOURSELF

○ Shower and brush teeth and hair

○ Open a window, breathe in fresh air, and smile

○ Practice meditation or breathwork

○ Pray, sing, or dance

○ Other: _____

## FEEL YOUR FEELINGS

○ Today I feel _____

## ASK FOR SUPPORT

*Today I could use help with . . .*

○ Holding the baby while I shower or rest

○ Preparing food

○ Laundry and cleaning

○ Other: _____

Today I will ask for help from _____

# DAY 44

Time in nature can be a great reset when stress comes to call or you feel overwhelmed. Next time you can get outside, where will you go, and what will you do?

_____

_____

_____

_____

_____

_____

_____

_____

_____

_____

_____

_____

_____

_____

_____

_____

_____

_____

_____

_____

# SELF-CARE CHECKLIST

*Check the ways you've taken care of*
*(or intend to take care of) yourself today:*

## REST DEEPLY

○ Prioritize nighttime sleep

○ Nap when the baby naps at least once a day

## EAT MINDFULLY

○ Nourish yourself with healthy meals and snacks

○ Drink plenty of water

## HONOR RELATIONSHIPS

○ Connect with your partner, a close friend, or a relative

○ Text or call a friend

## MOVE YOUR BEAUTIFUL BODY

○ Stretch in bed

○ Practice gentle yoga or Pilates

## BE KIND TO YOURSELF

○ Shower and brush teeth and hair

○ Open a window, breathe in fresh air, and smile

○ Practice meditation or breathwork

○ Pray, sing, or dance

○ Other: _____

## FEEL YOUR FEELINGS

○ Today I feel _____

## ASK FOR SUPPORT

*Today I could use help with . . .*

○ Holding the baby while I shower or rest

○ Preparing food

○ Laundry and cleaning

○ Other: _____

Today I will ask for help from _____

# DAY 45

Spend some time thinking about and feeling into all that you're learning right now and then complete these sentences.

Motherhood is teaching me _____

_____

_____

_____

_____

_____

_____


What I love about motherhood is _____

_____

_____

_____

_____

_____

_____

_____

# SELF-CARE CHECKLIST

*Check the ways you've taken care of*
*(or intend to take care of) yourself today:*

## REST DEEPLY

○ Prioritize nighttime sleep

○ Nap when the baby naps at least once a day

## EAT MINDFULLY

○ Nourish yourself with healthy meals and snacks

○ Drink plenty of water

## HONOR RELATIONSHIPS

○ Connect with your partner, a close friend, or a relative

○ Text or call a friend

## MOVE YOUR BEAUTIFUL BODY

○ Stretch in bed

○ Practice gentle yoga or Pilates

## BE KIND TO YOURSELF

○ Shower and brush teeth and hair

○ Open a window, breathe in fresh air, and smile

○ Practice meditation or breathwork

○ Pray, sing, or dance

○ Other: _____

## FEEL YOUR FEELINGS

○ Today I feel _____

## ASK FOR SUPPORT

*Today I could use help with . . .*

○ Holding the baby while I shower or rest

○ Preparing food

○ Laundry and cleaning

○ Other: _____

Today I will ask for help from _____

# DAY 46

When things feel hard, it can help to acknowledge the feelings and then practice some self-care. Write down what's been hard for you lately and one thing you can do to nourish yourself.

# SELF-CARE CHECKLIST

*Check the ways you've taken care of*
*(or intend to take care of) yourself today:*

## REST DEEPLY

- ○ Prioritize nighttime sleep
- ○ Nap when the baby naps at least once a day

## EAT MINDFULLY

- ○ Nourish yourself with healthy meals and snacks
- ○ Drink plenty of water

## HONOR RELATIONSHIPS

- ○ Connect with your partner, a close friend, or a relative
- ○ Text or call a friend

## MOVE YOUR BEAUTIFUL BODY

- ○ Stretch in bed
- ○ Practice gentle yoga or Pilates

## BE KIND TO YOURSELF

- ○ Shower and brush teeth and hair
- ○ Practice meditation or breathwork
- ○ Open a window, breathe in fresh air, and smile
- ○ Pray, sing, or dance
- ○ Other: _____

## FEEL YOUR FEELINGS

- ○ Today I feel _____

## ASK FOR SUPPORT

*Today I could use help with . . .*

- ○ Holding the baby while I shower or rest
- ○ Laundry and cleaning
- ○ Other: _____
- ○ Preparing food

Today I will ask for help from _____

# DAY 47

Notice if you feel preoccupied with how you "should" look post-partum. Give yourself some space and grace here. How do you want to feel in this new body of yours?

_____

_____

_____

_____

_____

_____

_____

_____

_____

_____

_____

_____

_____

_____

_____

_____

_____

_____

_____

# SELF-CARE CHECKLIST

*Check the ways you've taken care of*
*(or intend to take care of) yourself today:*

## REST DEEPLY

○ Prioritize nighttime sleep

○ Nap when the baby naps at least once a day

## EAT MINDFULLY

○ Nourish yourself with healthy meals and snacks

○ Drink plenty of water

## HONOR RELATIONSHIPS

○ Connect with your partner, a close friend, or a relative

○ Text or call a friend

## MOVE YOUR BEAUTIFUL BODY

○ Stretch in bed

○ Practice gentle yoga or Pilates

## BE KIND TO YOURSELF

○ Shower and brush teeth and hair

○ Open a window, breathe in fresh air, and smile

○ Practice meditation or breathwork

○ Pray, sing, or dance

○ Other: _____

## FEEL YOUR FEELINGS

○ Today I feel _____

## ASK FOR SUPPORT

*Today I could use help with . . .*

○ Holding the baby while I shower or rest

○ Preparing food

○ Laundry and cleaning

○ Other: _____

Today I will ask for help from _____

# DAY 48

Write a love note to yourself.

**Dear self, today I just want you to know that** _____

_____

_____

_____

_____

_____

_____

_____

_____

_____

_____

_____

_____

_____

_____

_____

_____

_____

_____

_____

_____

# SELF-CARE CHECKLIST

*Check the ways you've taken care of
(or intend to take care of) yourself today:*

## REST DEEPLY

○ Prioritize nighttime sleep

○ Nap when the baby naps at least once a day

## EAT MINDFULLY

○ Nourish yourself with healthy meals and snacks

○ Drink plenty of water

## HONOR RELATIONSHIPS

○ Connect with your partner, a close friend, or a relative

○ Text or call a friend

## MOVE YOUR BEAUTIFUL BODY

○ Stretch in bed

○ Practice gentle yoga or Pilates

## BE KIND TO YOURSELF

○ Shower and brush teeth and hair

○ Open a window, breathe in fresh air, and smile

○ Practice meditation or breathwork

○ Pray, sing, or dance

○ Other: _____

## FEEL YOUR FEELINGS

○ Today I feel _____

## ASK FOR SUPPORT

*Today I could use help with . . .*

○ Holding the baby while I shower or rest

○ Preparing food

○ Laundry and cleaning

○ Other: _____

Today I will ask for help from _____

# DAY 49

What adults have you interacted with lately? Write down three people you can call, text, or invite over this week so you can have some much-needed adult time.

1. _____
   _____
   _____
   _____
   _____

2. _____
   _____
   _____
   _____
   _____

3. _____
   _____
   _____
   _____

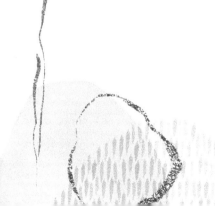

# SELF-CARE CHECKLIST

*Check the ways you've taken care of*
*(or intend to take care of) yourself today:*

## REST DEEPLY

○ Prioritize nighttime sleep

○ Nap when the baby naps at least once a day

## EAT MINDFULLY

○ Nourish yourself with healthy meals and snacks

○ Drink plenty of water

## HONOR RELATIONSHIPS

○ Connect with your partner, a close friend, or a relative

○ Text or call a friend

## MOVE YOUR BEAUTIFUL BODY

○ Stretch in bed

○ Practice gentle yoga or Pilates

## BE KIND TO YOURSELF

○ Shower and brush teeth and hair

○ Open a window, breathe in fresh air, and smile

○ Practice meditation or breathwork

○ Pray, sing, or dance

○ Other: _____

## FEEL YOUR FEELINGS

○ Today I feel _____

## ASK FOR SUPPORT

*Today I could use help with . . .*

○ Holding the baby while I shower or rest

○ Preparing food

○ Laundry and cleaning

○ Other: _____

Today I will ask for help from _____

# DAY 50

Cultivate intuition. The more you listen to and act on your inner wisdom, the more it grows. What is your inner voice whispering *(or perhaps shouting)* today?

_____

_____

_____

_____

_____

_____

_____

_____

_____

_____

_____

_____

_____

_____

_____

_____

_____

# SELF-CARE CHECKLIST

*Check the ways you've taken care of*
*(or intend to take care of) yourself today:*

## REST DEEPLY

○ Prioritize nighttime sleep

○ Nap when the baby naps at least once a day

## EAT MINDFULLY

○ Nourish yourself with healthy meals and snacks

○ Drink plenty of water

## HONOR RELATIONSHIPS

○ Connect with your partner, a close friend, or a relative

○ Text or call a friend

## MOVE YOUR BEAUTIFUL BODY

○ Stretch in bed

○ Practice gentle yoga or Pilates

## BE KIND TO YOURSELF

○ Shower and brush teeth and hair

○ Open a window, breathe in fresh air, and smile

○ Practice meditation or breathwork

○ Pray, sing, or dance

○ Other: _____

## FEEL YOUR FEELINGS

○ Today I feel _____

## ASK FOR SUPPORT

*Today I could use help with . . .*

○ Holding the baby while I shower or rest

○ Preparing food

○ Laundry and cleaning

○ Other: _____

Today I will ask for help from _____

# DAY 51

You can do hard things. Think of a positive affirmation that will get you through the tough days, and write it down five times (e.g., *"Today is hard, I can do this. I don't have to be perfect, I only have to do my best."*).

1. _____

_____

_____

2. _____

_____

_____

3. _____

_____

_____

4. _____

_____

_____

5. _____

_____

_____

# SELF-CARE CHECKLIST

*Check the ways you've taken care of
(or intend to take care of) yourself today:*

## REST DEEPLY

- ○ Prioritize nighttime sleep
- ○ Nap when the baby naps at least once a day

## EAT MINDFULLY

- ○ Nourish yourself with healthy meals and snacks
- ○ Drink plenty of water

## HONOR RELATIONSHIPS

- ○ Connect with your partner, a close friend, or a relative
- ○ Text or call a friend

## MOVE YOUR BEAUTIFUL BODY

- ○ Stretch in bed
- ○ Practice gentle yoga or Pilates

## BE KIND TO YOURSELF

- ○ Shower and brush teeth and hair
- ○ Practice meditation or breathwork
- ○ Open a window, breathe in fresh air, and smile
- ○ Pray, sing, or dance
- ○ Other: _____

## FEEL YOUR FEELINGS

- ○ Today I feel _____

## ASK FOR SUPPORT

*Today I could use help with . . .*

- ○ Holding the baby while I shower or rest
- ○ Laundry and cleaning
- ○ Other: _____
- ○ Preparing food

Today I will ask for help from _____

# DAY 52

As a new mom, it's natural to worry about everything *(Is my baby breathing? Are they gaining enough weight?)*. What are your biggest concerns right now? Who can help you problem-solve these concerns?

_____

_____

_____

_____

_____

_____

_____

_____

_____

_____

_____

_____

_____

_____

_____

_____

_____

# SELF-CARE CHECKLIST

*Check the ways you've taken care of
(or intend to take care of) yourself today:*

## REST DEEPLY

○ Prioritize nighttime sleep

○ Nap when the baby naps at least once a day

## EAT MINDFULLY

○ Nourish yourself with healthy meals and snacks

○ Drink plenty of water

## HONOR RELATIONSHIPS

○ Connect with your partner, a close friend, or a relative

○ Text or call a friend

## MOVE YOUR BEAUTIFUL BODY

○ Stretch in bed

○ Practice gentle yoga or Pilates

## BE KIND TO YOURSELF

○ Shower and brush teeth and hair

○ Open a window, breathe in fresh air, and smile

○ Practice meditation or breathwork

○ Pray, sing, or dance

○ Other: _____

## FEEL YOUR FEELINGS

○ Today I feel _____

## ASK FOR SUPPORT

*Today I could use help with . . .*

○ Holding the baby while I shower or rest

○ Preparing food

○ Laundry and cleaning

○ Other: _____

Today I will ask for help from _____

# DAY 53

Make a list of five simple pleasures that you look forward to enjoying again soon *(sunshine, intimacy with your partner or self, chocolate, a hot bath, etc.).*

1. _____

_____

_____

2. _____

_____

_____

3. _____

_____

_____

4. _____

_____

_____

5. _____

_____

_____

# SELF-CARE CHECKLIST

*Check the ways you've taken care of*
*(or intend to take care of) yourself today:*

## REST DEEPLY

○ Prioritize nighttime sleep

○ Nap when the baby naps at least once a day

## EAT MINDFULLY

○ Nourish yourself with healthy meals and snacks

○ Drink plenty of water

## HONOR RELATIONSHIPS

○ Connect with your partner, a close friend, or a relative

○ Text or call a friend

## MOVE YOUR BEAUTIFUL BODY

○ Stretch in bed

○ Practice gentle yoga or Pilates

## BE KIND TO YOURSELF

○ Shower and brush teeth and hair

○ Open a window, breathe in fresh air, and smile

○ Practice meditation or breathwork

○ Pray, sing, or dance

○ Other: _____

## FEEL YOUR FEELINGS

○ Today I feel _____

## ASK FOR SUPPORT

*Today I could use help with . . .*

○ Holding the baby while I shower or rest

○ Preparing food

○ Laundry and cleaning

○ Other: _____

Today I will ask for help from _____

# DAY 54

Practice gratitude. Place one hand over your heart and the other hand on your belly. Take a few deep breaths. Now gently say to yourself, "thank you," and write down five things you're grateful for.

1. _____
   _____
   _____

2. _____
   _____
   _____

3. _____
   _____
   _____

4. _____
   _____
   _____

5. _____
   _____
   _____

# SELF-CARE CHECKLIST

*Check the ways you've taken care of*
*(or intend to take care of) yourself today:*

## REST DEEPLY

○ Prioritize nighttime sleep

○ Nap when the baby naps at least once a day

## EAT MINDFULLY

○ Nourish yourself with healthy meals and snacks

○ Drink plenty of water

## HONOR RELATIONSHIPS

○ Connect with your partner, a close friend, or a relative

○ Text or call a friend

## MOVE YOUR BEAUTIFUL BODY

○ Stretch in bed

○ Practice gentle yoga or Pilates

## BE KIND TO YOURSELF

○ Shower and brush teeth and hair

○ Open a window, breathe in fresh air, and smile

○ Practice meditation or breathwork

○ Pray, sing, or dance

○ Other: _____

## FEEL YOUR FEELINGS

○ Today I feel _____

## ASK FOR SUPPORT

*Today I could use help with . . .*

○ Holding the baby while I shower or rest

○ Preparing food

○ Laundry and cleaning

○ Other: _____

Today I will ask for help from _____

# DAY 55

Social media can make motherhood look glamorous and easy.
Real life? Not so much. Reflect on how you feel when you scroll.
Does it feel nurturing and supportive, or does it cause anxiety
and feel draining? *(Gentle reminder: It's okay to unfollow accounts that
make you feel bad.)*

_____

_____

_____

_____

_____

_____

_____

_____

_____

_____

_____

_____

_____

_____

_____

_____

_____

_____

# SELF-CARE CHECKLIST

*Check the ways you've taken care of
(or intend to take care of) yourself today:*

## REST DEEPLY

- ○ Prioritize nighttime sleep
- ○ Nap when the baby naps at least once a day

## EAT MINDFULLY

- ○ Nourish yourself with healthy meals and snacks
- ○ Drink plenty of water

## HONOR RELATIONSHIPS

- ○ Connect with your partner, a close friend, or a relative
- ○ Text or call a friend

## MOVE YOUR BEAUTIFUL BODY

- ○ Stretch in bed
- ○ Practice gentle yoga or Pilates

## BE KIND TO YOURSELF

- ○ Shower and brush teeth and hair
- ○ Practice meditation or breathwork
- ○ Open a window, breathe in fresh air, and smile
- ○ Pray, sing, or dance
- ○ Other: _____

## FEEL YOUR FEELINGS

- ○ Today I feel _____

## ASK FOR SUPPORT

*Today I could use help with . . .*

- ○ Holding the baby while I shower or rest
- ○ Laundry and cleaning
- ○ Other: _____
- ○ Preparing food

Today I will ask for help from _____

# DAY 56

How do you make sense of motherhood? Is there a great spiritual purpose or meaning? How do you feel about being able to create a human?

_____

_____

_____

_____

_____

_____

_____

_____

_____

_____

_____

_____

_____

_____

_____

_____

_____

_____

_____

_____

_____

_____

# SELF-CARE CHECKLIST

*Check the ways you've taken care of
(or intend to take care of) yourself today:*

## REST DEEPLY

○ Prioritize nighttime sleep

○ Nap when the baby naps at least once a day

## EAT MINDFULLY

○ Nourish yourself with healthy meals and snacks

○ Drink plenty of water

## HONOR RELATIONSHIPS

○ Connect with your partner, a close friend, or a relative

○ Text or call a friend

## MOVE YOUR BEAUTIFUL BODY

○ Stretch in bed

○ Practice gentle yoga or Pilates

## BE KIND TO YOURSELF

○ Shower and brush teeth and hair

○ Open a window, breathe in fresh air, and smile

○ Practice meditation or breathwork

○ Pray, sing, or dance

○ Other: _____

## FEEL YOUR FEELINGS

○ Today I feel _____

## ASK FOR SUPPORT

*Today I could use help with . . .*

○ Holding the baby while I shower or rest

○ Preparing food

○ Laundry and cleaning

○ Other: _____

Today I will ask for help from _____

# DAY 57

Take time for yourself. Make a list of all the things you want or need. *(They don't have to be achievable today.)*

_____

_____

_____

_____

_____

_____

_____

_____

_____

_____

_____

_____

_____

_____

Now complete this sentence.

Today, what I need most is _____

_____

_____

# SELF-CARE CHECKLIST

*Check the ways you've taken care of
(or intend to take care of) yourself today:*

## REST DEEPLY

○ Prioritize nighttime sleep

○ Nap when the baby naps at least once a day

## EAT MINDFULLY

○ Nourish yourself with healthy meals and snacks

○ Drink plenty of water

## HONOR RELATIONSHIPS

○ Connect with your partner, a close friend, or a relative

○ Text or call a friend

## MOVE YOUR BEAUTIFUL BODY

○ Stretch in bed

○ Practice gentle yoga or Pilates

## BE KIND TO YOURSELF

○ Shower and brush teeth and hair

○ Open a window, breathe in fresh air, and smile

○ Practice meditation or breathwork

○ Pray, sing, or dance

○ Other: _____

## FEEL YOUR FEELINGS

○ Today I feel _____

## ASK FOR SUPPORT

*Today I could use help with . . .*

○ Holding the baby while I shower or rest

○ Preparing food

○ Laundry and cleaning

○ Other: _____

Today I will ask for help from _____

# DAY 58

The practice of nurturing yourself as a new mom is an art. Are you being kind to yourself as you grow and learn? List three things you've learned so far about yourself and about being a mom.

1. _____
   _____
   _____
   _____
   _____

2. _____
   _____
   _____
   _____
   _____

3. _____
   _____
   _____
   _____
   _____

# SELF-CARE CHECKLIST

*Check the ways you've taken care of*
*(or intend to take care of) yourself today:*

## REST DEEPLY

○ Prioritize nighttime sleep

○ Nap when the baby naps at least once a day

## EAT MINDFULLY

○ Nourish yourself with healthy meals and snacks

○ Drink plenty of water

## HONOR RELATIONSHIPS

○ Connect with your partner, a close friend, or a relative

○ Text or call a friend

## MOVE YOUR BEAUTIFUL BODY

○ Stretch in bed

○ Practice gentle yoga or Pilates

## BE KIND TO YOURSELF

○ Shower and brush teeth and hair

○ Open a window, breathe in fresh air, and smile

○ Practice meditation or breathwork

○ Pray, sing, or dance

○ Other: _____

## FEEL YOUR FEELINGS

○ Today I feel _____

## ASK FOR SUPPORT

*Today I could use help with . . .*

○ Holding the baby while I shower or rest

○ Preparing food

○ Laundry and cleaning

○ Other: _____

Today I will ask for help from _____

# DAY 59

Look within. Notice your mind thinking, your body breathing, and your heart feeling. You don't have to stop your thoughts to find peace. What does it feel like to just observe yourself and do nothing?

_____

_____

_____

_____

_____

_____

_____

_____

_____

_____

_____

_____

_____

_____

_____

_____

_____

# SELF-CARE CHECKLIST

*Check the ways you've taken care of*
*(or intend to take care of) yourself today:*

## REST DEEPLY

○ Prioritize nighttime sleep

○ Nap when the baby naps at least once a day

## EAT MINDFULLY

○ Nourish yourself with healthy meals and snacks

○ Drink plenty of water

## HONOR RELATIONSHIPS

○ Connect with your partner, a close friend, or a relative

○ Text or call a friend

## MOVE YOUR BEAUTIFUL BODY

○ Stretch in bed

○ Practice gentle yoga or Pilates

## BE KIND TO YOURSELF

○ Shower and brush teeth and hair

○ Open a window, breathe in fresh air, and smile

○ Practice meditation or breathwork

○ Pray, sing, or dance

○ Other: _____

## FEEL YOUR FEELINGS

○ Today I feel _____

## ASK FOR SUPPORT

*Today I could use help with . . .*

○ Holding the baby while I shower or rest

○ Preparing food

○ Laundry and cleaning

○ Other: _____

Today I will ask for help from _____

# DAY 60

List the top three supportive people, books, blogs, or resources you turn to and trust for motherhood advice.

1. _____

_____

_____

_____

_____

2. _____

_____

_____

_____

_____

3. _____

_____

_____

_____

_____

# SELF-CARE CHECKLIST

*Check the ways you've taken care of*
*(or intend to take care of) yourself today:*

## REST DEEPLY

○ Prioritize nighttime sleep

○ Nap when the baby naps at least once a day

## EAT MINDFULLY

○ Nourish yourself with healthy meals and snacks

○ Drink plenty of water

## HONOR RELATIONSHIPS

○ Connect with your partner, a close friend, or a relative

○ Text or call a friend

## MOVE YOUR BEAUTIFUL BODY

○ Stretch in bed

○ Practice gentle yoga or Pilates

## BE KIND TO YOURSELF

○ Shower and brush teeth and hair

○ Open a window, breathe in fresh air, and smile

○ Practice meditation or breathwork

○ Pray, sing, or dance

○ Other: _____

## FEEL YOUR FEELINGS

○ Today I feel _____

## ASK FOR SUPPORT

*Today I could use help with . . .*

○ Holding the baby while I shower or rest

○ Preparing food

○ Laundry and cleaning

○ Other: _____

Today I will ask for help from _____

# DAY 61

List three people, books, blogs, or resources that stress you out and make you feel like a "bad mom." *(Give yourself permission to unfriend/unfollow, donate the book, or never check that website again.)*

1. _____

_____

_____

_____

_____

2. _____

_____

_____

_____

_____

3. _____

_____

_____

_____

_____

# SELF-CARE CHECKLIST

*Check the ways you've taken care of
(or intend to take care of) yourself today:*

## REST DEEPLY

○ Prioritize nighttime sleep

○ Nap when the baby naps at least once a day

## EAT MINDFULLY

○ Nourish yourself with healthy meals and snacks

○ Drink plenty of water

## HONOR RELATIONSHIPS

○ Connect with your partner, a close friend, or a relative

○ Text or call a friend

## MOVE YOUR BEAUTIFUL BODY

○ Stretch in bed

○ Practice gentle yoga or Pilates

## BE KIND TO YOURSELF

○ Shower and brush teeth and hair

○ Open a window, breathe in fresh air, and smile

○ Practice meditation or breathwork

○ Pray, sing, or dance

○ Other: _____

## FEEL YOUR FEELINGS

○ Today I feel _____

## ASK FOR SUPPORT

*Today I could use help with . . .*

○ Holding the baby while I shower or rest

○ Preparing food

○ Laundry and cleaning

○ Other: _____

Today I will ask for help from _____

# DAY 62

How have you navigated maternity leave options, going back to work, or continuing to stay at home? How do you feel about your decision?

_____

_____

_____

_____

_____

_____

_____

_____

_____

_____

_____

_____

_____

_____

_____

_____

# SELF-CARE CHECKLIST

*Check the ways you've taken care of*
*(or intend to take care of) yourself today:*

## REST DEEPLY

○ Prioritize nighttime sleep

○ Nap when the baby naps at least once a day

## EAT MINDFULLY

○ Nourish yourself with healthy meals and snacks

○ Drink plenty of water

## HONOR RELATIONSHIPS

○ Connect with your partner, a close friend, or a relative

○ Text or call a friend

## MOVE YOUR BEAUTIFUL BODY

○ Stretch in bed

○ Practice gentle yoga or Pilates

## BE KIND TO YOURSELF

○ Shower and brush teeth and hair

○ Open a window, breathe in fresh air, and smile

○ Practice meditation or breathwork

○ Pray, sing, or dance

○ Other: _____

## FEEL YOUR FEELINGS

○ Today I feel _____

## ASK FOR SUPPORT

*Today I could use help with . . .*

○ Holding the baby while I shower or rest

○ Preparing food

○ Laundry and cleaning

○ Other: _____

Today I will ask for help from _____

# DAY 63

Slow down, mama. Inhale for four counts, and exhale for four counts. Make a list of five things you can do slowly today.

1. _____
   _____
   _____

2. _____
   _____
   _____

3. _____
   _____
   _____

4. _____
   _____
   _____

5. _____
   _____
   _____

# SELF-CARE CHECKLIST

*Check the ways you've taken care of*
*(or intend to take care of) yourself today:*

## REST DEEPLY

○ Prioritize nighttime sleep

○ Nap when the baby naps at least once a day

## EAT MINDFULLY

○ Nourish yourself with healthy meals and snacks

○ Drink plenty of water

## HONOR RELATIONSHIPS

○ Connect with your partner, a close friend, or a relative

○ Text or call a friend

## MOVE YOUR BEAUTIFUL BODY

○ Stretch in bed

○ Practice gentle yoga or Pilates

## BE KIND TO YOURSELF

○ Shower and brush teeth and hair

○ Open a window, breathe in fresh air, and smile

○ Practice meditation or breathwork

○ Pray, sing, or dance

○ Other: _____

## FEEL YOUR FEELINGS

○ Today I feel _____

## ASK FOR SUPPORT

*Today I could use help with . . .*

○ Holding the baby while I shower or rest

○ Preparing food

○ Laundry and cleaning

○ Other: _____

Today I will ask for help from _____

# DAY 64

Becoming a mother reconnects you with your own experience of being mothered. What did you learn from your mother that you'd like to bring with you on this journey? What would you like to leave behind?

_____

_____

_____

_____

_____

_____

_____

_____

_____

_____

_____

_____

_____

_____

_____

_____

_____

_____

# SELF-CARE CHECKLIST

*Check the ways you've taken care of*
*(or intend to take care of) yourself today:*

## REST DEEPLY

○ Prioritize nighttime sleep

○ Nap when the baby naps at least once a day

## EAT MINDFULLY

○ Nourish yourself with healthy meals and snacks

○ Drink plenty of water

## HONOR RELATIONSHIPS

○ Connect with your partner, a close friend, or a relative

○ Text or call a friend

## MOVE YOUR BEAUTIFUL BODY

○ Stretch in bed

○ Practice gentle yoga or Pilates

## BE KIND TO YOURSELF

○ Shower and brush teeth and hair

○ Open a window, breathe in fresh air, and smile

○ Practice meditation or breathwork

○ Pray, sing, or dance

○ Other: _____

## FEEL YOUR FEELINGS

○ Today I feel _____

## ASK FOR SUPPORT

*Today I could use help with . . .*

○ Holding the baby while I shower or rest

○ Preparing food

○ Laundry and cleaning

○ Other: _____

Today I will ask for help from _____

# DAY 65

Having a bad day doesn't make you a "bad mom." Be mindful of how you talk to yourself when you stumble. List three nice things you can say to yourself when the day is challenging (e.g., *"Motherhood is hard for everyone, not just me. Today sucked, tomorrow will be better. I'm feeling overwhelmed, that just means I need more support."*).

1. _____

_____

_____

_____

_____

2. _____

_____

_____

_____

_____

3. _____

_____

_____

_____

_____

# SELF-CARE CHECKLIST

*Check the ways you've taken care of*
*(or intend to take care of) yourself today:*

## REST DEEPLY

○ Prioritize nighttime sleep

○ Nap when the baby naps at least once a day

## EAT MINDFULLY

○ Nourish yourself with healthy meals and snacks

○ Drink plenty of water

## HONOR RELATIONSHIPS

○ Connect with your partner, a close friend, or a relative

○ Text or call a friend

## MOVE YOUR BEAUTIFUL BODY

○ Stretch in bed

○ Practice gentle yoga or Pilates

## BE KIND TO YOURSELF

○ Shower and brush teeth and hair

○ Practice meditation or breathwork

○ Open a window, breathe in fresh air, and smile

○ Pray, sing, or dance

○ Other: _____

## FEEL YOUR FEELINGS

○ Today I feel _____

## ASK FOR SUPPORT

*Today I could use help with . . .*

○ Holding the baby while I shower or rest

○ Laundry and cleaning

○ Other: _____

○ Preparing food

Today I will ask for help from _____

# DAY 66

Motherhood can be lonely. Cultivate community by connecting with local mom groups for meetups and mommy-and-me classes. Have a look online and list three classes or groups you are interested in joining.

1. _____

_____

_____

_____

2. _____

_____

_____

_____

3. _____

_____

_____

_____

# SELF-CARE CHECKLIST

*Check the ways you've taken care of
(or intend to take care of) yourself today:*

## REST DEEPLY

○ Prioritize nighttime sleep

○ Nap when the baby naps at least once a day

## EAT MINDFULLY

○ Nourish yourself with healthy meals and snacks

○ Drink plenty of water

## HONOR RELATIONSHIPS

○ Connect with your partner, a close friend, or a relative

○ Text or call a friend

## MOVE YOUR BEAUTIFUL BODY

○ Stretch in bed

○ Practice gentle yoga or Pilates

## BE KIND TO YOURSELF

○ Shower and brush teeth and hair

○ Open a window, breathe in fresh air, and smile

○ Practice meditation or breathwork

○ Pray, sing, or dance

○ Other: _____

## FEEL YOUR FEELINGS

○ Today I feel _____

## ASK FOR SUPPORT

*Today I could use help with . . .*

○ Holding the baby while I shower or rest

○ Preparing food

○ Laundry and cleaning

○ Other: _____

Today I will ask for help from _____

# DAY 67

Do something extra kind for yourself today. What feels like an attainable luxury? Make a list of five ideas and pick one thing to make happen for yourself today.

1. _____
_____
_____

2. _____
_____
_____

3. _____
_____
_____

4. _____
_____
_____

5. _____
_____
_____

# SELF-CARE CHECKLIST

*Check the ways you've taken care of
(or intend to take care of) yourself today:*

## REST DEEPLY

○ Prioritize nighttime sleep

○ Nap when the baby naps at least once a day

## EAT MINDFULLY

○ Nourish yourself with healthy meals and snacks

○ Drink plenty of water

## HONOR RELATIONSHIPS

○ Connect with your partner, a close friend, or a relative

○ Text or call a friend

## MOVE YOUR BEAUTIFUL BODY

○ Stretch in bed

○ Practice gentle yoga or Pilates

## BE KIND TO YOURSELF

○ Shower and brush teeth and hair

○ Open a window, breathe in fresh air, and smile

○ Practice meditation or breathwork

○ Pray, sing, or dance

○ Other: _____

## FEEL YOUR FEELINGS

○ Today I feel _____

## ASK FOR SUPPORT

*Today I could use help with . . .*

○ Holding the baby while I shower or rest

○ Preparing food

○ Laundry and cleaning

○ Other: _____

Today I will ask for help from _____

# DAY 68

Now that you've been carving out time for daily self-care, take a moment to reflect. Does it feel frivolous or necessary? Do you look forward to it, or does it feel like a chore?

_____

_____

_____

_____

_____

_____

_____

_____

_____

_____

_____

_____

_____

_____

_____

_____

# SELF-CARE CHECKLIST

*Check the ways you've taken care of
(or intend to take care of) yourself today:*

## REST DEEPLY

○ Prioritize nighttime sleep

○ Nap when the baby naps at least once a day

## EAT MINDFULLY

○ Nourish yourself with healthy meals and snacks

○ Drink plenty of water

## HONOR RELATIONSHIPS

○ Connect with your partner, a close friend, or a relative

○ Text or call a friend

## MOVE YOUR BEAUTIFUL BODY

○ Stretch in bed

○ Practice gentle yoga or Pilates

## BE KIND TO YOURSELF

○ Shower and brush teeth and hair

○ Open a window, breathe in fresh air, and smile

○ Practice meditation or breathwork

○ Pray, sing, or dance

○ Other: _____

## FEEL YOUR FEELINGS

○ Today I feel _____

## ASK FOR SUPPORT

*Today I could use help with . . .*

○ Holding the baby while I shower or rest

○ Preparing food

○ Laundry and cleaning

○ Other: _____

Today I will ask for help from _____

# DAY 69

Give yourself a hug. A real, wrap-your-arms-around-and-squeeze-with-a-big-smile hug. Reflect on how much you're learning. What are five things you appreciate about the motherhood journey thus far?

1. _____

_____

_____

2. _____

_____

_____

3. _____

_____

_____

4. _____

_____

_____

5. _____

_____

_____

# SELF-CARE CHECKLIST

*Check the ways you've taken care of*
*(or intend to take care of) yourself today:*

## REST DEEPLY

○ Prioritize nighttime sleep

○ Nap when the baby naps at least once a day

## EAT MINDFULLY

○ Nourish yourself with healthy meals and snacks

○ Drink plenty of water

## HONOR RELATIONSHIPS

○ Connect with your partner, a close friend, or a relative

○ Text or call a friend

## MOVE YOUR BEAUTIFUL BODY

○ Stretch in bed

○ Practice gentle yoga or Pilates

## BE KIND TO YOURSELF

○ Shower and brush teeth and hair

○ Open a window, breathe in fresh air, and smile

○ Practice meditation or breathwork

○ Pray, sing, or dance

○ Other: _____

## FEEL YOUR FEELINGS

○ Today I feel _____

## ASK FOR SUPPORT

*Today I could use help with . . .*

○ Holding the baby while I shower or rest

○ Preparing food

○ Laundry and cleaning

○ Other: _____

Today I will ask for help from _____

# DAY 70

Small steps have a big impact. Don't underestimate the power of a one-minute daily practice. Brainstorm three nourishing things you can do for yourself in just one minute *(child's pose, deep breathing, gratitude practice, etc.)*.

1. _____
   _____
   _____
   _____

2. _____
   _____
   _____
   _____
   _____

3. _____
   _____
   _____
   _____
   _____

# SELF-CARE CHECKLIST

*Check the ways you've taken care of*
*(or intend to take care of) yourself today:*

## REST DEEPLY

○ Prioritize nighttime sleep

○ Nap when the baby naps at least once a day

## EAT MINDFULLY

○ Nourish yourself with healthy meals and snacks

○ Drink plenty of water

## HONOR RELATIONSHIPS

○ Connect with your partner, a close friend, or a relative

○ Text or call a friend

## MOVE YOUR BEAUTIFUL BODY

○ Stretch in bed

○ Practice gentle yoga or Pilates

## BE KIND TO YOURSELF

○ Shower and brush teeth and hair

○ Open a window, breathe in fresh air, and smile

○ Practice meditation or breathwork

○ Pray, sing, or dance

○ Other: _____

## FEEL YOUR FEELINGS

○ Today I feel _____

## ASK FOR SUPPORT

*Today I could use help with . . .*

○ Holding the baby while I shower or rest

○ Preparing food

○ Laundry and cleaning

○ Other: _____

Today I will ask for help from _____

# DAY 71

Mom guilt says, "You're not doing enough." To calm this inner mean girl, slow down and take a deep breath. Say out loud: "I've got this." Write down what you "got right" today. *(P.S. You're definitely doing enough.)*

_____

_____

_____

_____

_____

_____

_____

_____

_____

_____

_____

_____

_____

_____

_____

_____

_____

# SELF-CARE CHECKLIST

*Check the ways you've taken care of*
*(or intend to take care of) yourself today:*

## REST DEEPLY

○ Prioritize nighttime sleep

○ Nap when the baby naps at least once a day

## EAT MINDFULLY

○ Nourish yourself with healthy meals and snacks

○ Drink plenty of water

## HONOR RELATIONSHIPS

○ Connect with your partner, a close friend, or a relative

○ Text or call a friend

## MOVE YOUR BEAUTIFUL BODY

○ Stretch in bed

○ Practice gentle yoga or Pilates

## BE KIND TO YOURSELF

○ Shower and brush teeth and hair

○ Open a window, breathe in fresh air, and smile

○ Practice meditation or breathwork

○ Pray, sing, or dance

○ Other: _____

## FEEL YOUR FEELINGS

○ Today I feel _____

## ASK FOR SUPPORT

*Today I could use help with . . .*

○ Holding the baby while I shower or rest

○ Preparing food

○ Laundry and cleaning

○ Other: _____

Today I will ask for help from _____

# DAY 72

Developing self-compassion and positive self-talk is a practice. What are three kind things you can say to yourself today? *(e.g.,"I appreciate everything you do. I'm glad you're here.")*

1. _____

_____

_____

_____

_____

2. _____

_____

_____

_____

_____

3. _____

_____

_____

_____

_____

# SELF-CARE CHECKLIST

*Check the ways you've taken care of
(or intend to take care of) yourself today:*

## REST DEEPLY

○ Prioritize nighttime sleep

○ Nap when the baby naps at least once a day

## EAT MINDFULLY

○ Nourish yourself with healthy meals and snacks

○ Drink plenty of water

## HONOR RELATIONSHIPS

○ Connect with your partner, a close friend, or a relative

○ Text or call a friend

## MOVE YOUR BEAUTIFUL BODY

○ Stretch in bed

○ Practice gentle yoga or Pilates

## BE KIND TO YOURSELF

○ Shower and brush teeth and hair

○ Open a window, breathe in fresh air, and smile

○ Practice meditation or breathwork

○ Pray, sing, or dance

○ Other: _____

## FEEL YOUR FEELINGS

○ Today I feel _____

## ASK FOR SUPPORT

*Today I could use help with . . .*

○ Holding the baby while I shower or rest

○ Preparing food

○ Laundry and cleaning

○ Other: _____

Today I will ask for help from _____

# DAY 73

Sleep is foundational to your health and well-being, and chronic sleep deprivation can contribute to postpartum mood disorders. What are three ways you can get more rest during this intense time *(go to bed super early, take more naps on tough days, practice yoga nidra, etc.)*?

1. _____

_____

_____

_____

2. _____

_____

_____

_____

3. _____

_____

_____

_____

_____

# SELF-CARE CHECKLIST

*Check the ways you've taken care of*
*(or intend to take care of) yourself today:*

## REST DEEPLY

○ Prioritize nighttime sleep

○ Nap when the baby naps at least once a day

## EAT MINDFULLY

○ Nourish yourself with healthy meals and snacks

○ Drink plenty of water

## HONOR RELATIONSHIPS

○ Connect with your partner, a close friend, or a relative

○ Text or call a friend

## MOVE YOUR BEAUTIFUL BODY

○ Stretch in bed

○ Practice gentle yoga or Pilates

## BE KIND TO YOURSELF

○ Shower and brush teeth and hair

○ Open a window, breathe in fresh air, and smile

○ Practice meditation or breathwork

○ Pray, sing, or dance

○ Other: _____

## FEEL YOUR FEELINGS

○ Today I feel _____

## ASK FOR SUPPORT

*Today I could use help with . . .*

○ Holding the baby while I shower or rest

○ Preparing food

○ Laundry and cleaning

○ Other: _____

Today I will ask for help from _____

# DAY 74

Today, let yourself focus on your baby and all the day-to-day tasks that come along with caring for a newborn. Let the rest go. Write down all the tasks you can let go of and tackle another time.

# SELF-CARE CHECKLIST

*Check the ways you've taken care of*
*(or intend to take care of) yourself today:*

## REST DEEPLY

○ Prioritize nighttime sleep

○ Nap when the baby naps at least once a day

## EAT MINDFULLY

○ Nourish yourself with healthy meals and snacks

○ Drink plenty of water

## HONOR RELATIONSHIPS

○ Connect with your partner, a close friend, or a relative

○ Text or call a friend

## MOVE YOUR BEAUTIFUL BODY

○ Stretch in bed

○ Practice gentle yoga or Pilates

## BE KIND TO YOURSELF

○ Shower and brush teeth and hair

○ Open a window, breathe in fresh air, and smile

○ Practice meditation or breathwork

○ Pray, sing, or dance

○ Other: _____

## FEEL YOUR FEELINGS

○ Today I feel _____

## ASK FOR SUPPORT

*Today I could use help with . . .*

○ Holding the baby while I shower or rest

○ Preparing food

○ Laundry and cleaning

○ Other: _____

Today I will ask for help from _____

# DAY 75

Nourishing your beautiful body is a practice. What is your body craving today: more food, movement, connection, or quiet? How can you meet this need today?

_____

_____

_____

_____

_____

_____

_____

_____

_____

_____

_____

_____

_____

_____

_____

_____

_____

_____

_____

_____

# SELF-CARE CHECKLIST

*Check the ways you've taken care of*
*(or intend to take care of) yourself today:*

## REST DEEPLY

○ Prioritize nighttime sleep

○ Nap when the baby naps at least once a day

## EAT MINDFULLY

○ Nourish yourself with healthy meals and snacks

○ Drink plenty of water

## HONOR RELATIONSHIPS

○ Connect with your partner, a close friend, or a relative

○ Text or call a friend

## MOVE YOUR BEAUTIFUL BODY

○ Stretch in bed

○ Practice gentle yoga or Pilates

## BE KIND TO YOURSELF

○ Shower and brush teeth and hair

○ Open a window, breathe in fresh air, and smile

○ Practice meditation or breathwork

○ Pray, sing, or dance

○ Other: _____

## FEEL YOUR FEELINGS

○ Today I feel _____

## ASK FOR SUPPORT

*Today I could use help with . . .*

○ Holding the baby while I shower or rest

○ Preparing food

○ Laundry and cleaning

○ Other: _____

Today I will ask for help from _____

# DAY 76

You know more about mothering your baby than any book. Trust yourself. Make a list of the values and qualities of being a mom that are important to you.

_____

_____

_____

_____

_____

_____

_____

_____

_____

_____

_____

_____

_____

_____

_____

_____

_____

_____

_____

_____

# SELF-CARE CHECKLIST

*Check the ways you've taken care of*
*(or intend to take care of) yourself today:*

## REST DEEPLY

○ Prioritize nighttime sleep

○ Nap when the baby naps at least once a day

## EAT MINDFULLY

○ Nourish yourself with healthy meals and snacks

○ Drink plenty of water

## HONOR RELATIONSHIPS

○ Connect with your partner, a close friend, or a relative

○ Text or call a friend

## MOVE YOUR BEAUTIFUL BODY

○ Stretch in bed

○ Practice gentle yoga or Pilates

## BE KIND TO YOURSELF

○ Shower and brush teeth and hair

○ Open a window, breathe in fresh air, and smile

○ Practice meditation or breathwork

○ Pray, sing, or dance

○ Other: _____

## FEEL YOUR FEELINGS

○ Today I feel _____

## ASK FOR SUPPORT

*Today I could use help with . . .*

○ Holding the baby while I shower or rest

○ Preparing food

○ Laundry and cleaning

○ Other: _____

Today I will ask for help from _____

# DAY 77

Notice your feet on the ground and feel your body breathing.
What feels supportive and sacred in your life right now? What
routines or spiritual practices are working for you during this
chaotic time?

_____

_____

_____

_____

_____

_____

_____

_____

_____

_____

_____

_____

_____

_____

_____

_____

_____

# SELF-CARE CHECKLIST

*Check the ways you've taken care of*
*(or intend to take care of) yourself today:*

## REST DEEPLY

- ○ Prioritize nighttime sleep
- ○ Nap when the baby naps at least once a day

## EAT MINDFULLY

- ○ Nourish yourself with healthy meals and snacks
- ○ Drink plenty of water

## HONOR RELATIONSHIPS

- ○ Connect with your partner, a close friend, or a relative
- ○ Text or call a friend

## MOVE YOUR BEAUTIFUL BODY

- ○ Stretch in bed
- ○ Practice gentle yoga or Pilates

## BE KIND TO YOURSELF

- ○ Shower and brush teeth and hair
- ○ Practice meditation or breathwork
- ○ Open a window, breathe in fresh air, and smile
- ○ Pray, sing, or dance
- ○ Other: _____

## FEEL YOUR FEELINGS

- ○ Today I feel _____

## ASK FOR SUPPORT

*Today I could use help with . . .*

- ○ Holding the baby while I shower or rest
- ○ Laundry and cleaning
- ○ Other: _____
- ○ Preparing food

Today I will ask for help from _____

# DAY 78

Practice loving yourself as you are today. Complete the sentence.

**What I love about myself is** _____

_____

_____

_____

_____

_____

_____

_____

_____

_____

_____

_____

_____

_____

_____

_____

_____

_____

_____

_____

_____

# SELF-CARE CHECKLIST

*Check the ways you've taken care of*
*(or intend to take care of) yourself today:*

## REST DEEPLY

- ○ Prioritize nighttime sleep
- ○ Nap when the baby naps at least once a day

## EAT MINDFULLY

- ○ Nourish yourself with healthy meals and snacks
- ○ Drink plenty of water

## HONOR RELATIONSHIPS

- ○ Connect with your partner, a close friend, or a relative
- ○ Text or call a friend

## MOVE YOUR BEAUTIFUL BODY

- ○ Stretch in bed
- ○ Practice gentle yoga or Pilates

## BE KIND TO YOURSELF

- ○ Shower and brush teeth and hair
- ○ Practice meditation or breathwork
- ○ Open a window, breathe in fresh air, and smile
- ○ Pray, sing, or dance
- ○ Other: _____

## FEEL YOUR FEELINGS

- ○ Today I feel _____

## ASK FOR SUPPORT

*Today I could use help with . . .*

- ○ Holding the baby while I shower or rest
- ○ Laundry and cleaning
- ○ Other: _____
- ○ Preparing food

Today I will ask for help from _____

# DAY 79

Take a moment to envision your best self, confident in your ability to handle whatever motherhood brings your way. What does this version of you look like? What is she feeling and thinking?

_____

_____

_____

_____

_____

_____

_____

_____

_____

_____

_____

_____

_____

_____

_____

_____

_____

_____

_____

_____

# SELF-CARE CHECKLIST

*Check the ways you've taken care of*
*(or intend to take care of) yourself today:*

## REST DEEPLY

○ Prioritize nighttime sleep

○ Nap when the baby naps at least once a day

## EAT MINDFULLY

○ Nourish yourself with healthy meals and snacks

○ Drink plenty of water

## HONOR RELATIONSHIPS

○ Connect with your partner, a close friend, or a relative

○ Text or call a friend

## MOVE YOUR BEAUTIFUL BODY

○ Stretch in bed

○ Practice gentle yoga or Pilates

## BE KIND TO YOURSELF

○ Shower and brush teeth and hair

○ Open a window, breathe in fresh air, and smile

○ Practice meditation or breathwork

○ Pray, sing, or dance

○ Other: _____

## FEEL YOUR FEELINGS

○ Today I feel _____

## ASK FOR SUPPORT

*Today I could use help with . . .*

○ Holding the baby while I shower or rest

○ Preparing food

○ Laundry and cleaning

○ Other: _____

Today I will ask for help from _____

# DAY 80

Cultivate loving-kindness for yourself. List five things you are doing well as a new mama.

1. _____
_____
_____

2. _____
_____
_____

3. _____
_____
_____

4. _____
_____
_____

5. _____
_____
_____

# SELF-CARE CHECKLIST

*Check the ways you've taken care of
(or intend to take care of) yourself today:*

## REST DEEPLY

○ Prioritize nighttime sleep

○ Nap when the baby naps at least once a day

## EAT MINDFULLY

○ Nourish yourself with healthy meals and snacks

○ Drink plenty of water

## HONOR RELATIONSHIPS

○ Connect with your partner, a close friend, or a relative

○ Text or call a friend

## MOVE YOUR BEAUTIFUL BODY

○ Stretch in bed

○ Practice gentle yoga or Pilates

## BE KIND TO YOURSELF

○ Shower and brush teeth and hair

○ Open a window, breathe in fresh air, and smile

○ Practice meditation or breathwork

○ Pray, sing, or dance

○ Other: _____

## FEEL YOUR FEELINGS

○ Today I feel _____

## ASK FOR SUPPORT

*Today I could use help with . . .*

○ Holding the baby while I shower or rest

○ Preparing food

○ Laundry and cleaning

○ Other: _____

Today I will ask for help from _____

# DAY 81

It can be tempting to put off connecting with friends until you have more time to yourself. Free time can be scarce these days, but try to prioritize reaching out for connection and support. Name three people you want to reconnect with, and try a spontaneous catch-up call.

1. _____

_____

_____

_____

_____

2. _____

_____

_____

_____

_____

3. _____

_____

_____

_____

_____

# SELF-CARE CHECKLIST

*Check the ways you've taken care of*
*(or intend to take care of) yourself today:*

## REST DEEPLY

○ Prioritize nighttime sleep

○ Nap when the baby naps at least once a day

## EAT MINDFULLY

○ Nourish yourself with healthy meals and snacks

○ Drink plenty of water

## HONOR RELATIONSHIPS

○ Connect with your partner, a close friend, or a relative

○ Text or call a friend

## MOVE YOUR BEAUTIFUL BODY

○ Stretch in bed

○ Practice gentle yoga or Pilates

## BE KIND TO YOURSELF

○ Shower and brush teeth and hair

○ Open a window, breathe in fresh air, and smile

○ Practice meditation or breathwork

○ Pray, sing, or dance

○ Other: _____

## FEEL YOUR FEELINGS

○ Today I feel _____

## ASK FOR SUPPORT

*Today I could use help with . . .*

○ Holding the baby while I shower or rest

○ Preparing food

○ Laundry and cleaning

○ Other: _____

Today I will ask for help from _____

# DAY 82

Today is a good day to care for your body. Make a list of all the things that would feel nourishing to your body right now *(a long shower, shaving your legs, applying a face mask, etc.).*

_____

_____

_____

_____

_____

_____

_____

_____

_____

_____

_____

_____

_____

_____

_____

_____

_____

_____

_____

# SELF-CARE CHECKLIST

*Check the ways you've taken care of
(or intend to take care of) yourself today:*

## REST DEEPLY

○ Prioritize nighttime sleep

○ Nap when the baby naps at least once a day

## EAT MINDFULLY

○ Nourish yourself with healthy meals and snacks

○ Drink plenty of water

## HONOR RELATIONSHIPS

○ Connect with your partner, a close friend, or a relative

○ Text or call a friend

## MOVE YOUR BEAUTIFUL BODY

○ Stretch in bed

○ Practice gentle yoga or Pilates

## BE KIND TO YOURSELF

○ Shower and brush teeth and hair

○ Practice meditation or breathwork

○ Open a window, breathe in fresh air, and smile

○ Pray, sing, or dance

○ Other: _____

## FEEL YOUR FEELINGS

○ Today I feel _____

## ASK FOR SUPPORT

*Today I could use help with . . .*

○ Holding the baby while I shower or rest

○ Laundry and cleaning

○ Other: _____

○ Preparing food

Today I will ask for help from _____

# DAY 83

Orgasm is a powerful healer. Let yourself stay connected to your sexuality during this intense time. Do you feel connected or disconnected from your sexuality? How is it different now that you're a mom?

_____

_____

_____

_____

_____

_____

_____

_____

_____

_____

_____

_____

_____

_____

_____

_____

_____

_____

_____

# SELF-CARE CHECKLIST

*Check the ways you've taken care of
(or intend to take care of) yourself today:*

## REST DEEPLY

○ Prioritize nighttime sleep

○ Nap when the baby naps at least once a day

## EAT MINDFULLY

○ Nourish yourself with healthy meals and snacks

○ Drink plenty of water

## HONOR RELATIONSHIPS

○ Connect with your partner, a close friend, or a relative

○ Text or call a friend

## MOVE YOUR BEAUTIFUL BODY

○ Stretch in bed

○ Practice gentle yoga or Pilates

## BE KIND TO YOURSELF

○ Shower and brush teeth and hair

○ Practice meditation or breathwork

○ Open a window, breathe in fresh air, and smile

○ Pray, sing, or dance

○ Other: _____

## FEEL YOUR FEELINGS

○ Today I feel _____

## ASK FOR SUPPORT

*Today I could use help with . . .*

○ Holding the baby while I shower or rest

○ Laundry and cleaning

○ Other: _____

○ Preparing food

Today I will ask for help from _____

# DAY 84

Take time to move your body today. Head outside for some fresh air, try a gentle online yoga class, or have an epic dance party. Name five ways you can exercise while still recovering.

1. _____

_____

_____

2. _____

_____

_____

3. _____

_____

_____

4. _____

_____

_____

5. _____

_____

_____

# SELF-CARE CHECKLIST

*Check the ways you've taken care of
(or intend to take care of) yourself today:*

## REST DEEPLY

○ Prioritize nighttime sleep

○ Nap when the baby naps at least once a day

## EAT MINDFULLY

○ Nourish yourself with healthy meals and snacks

○ Drink plenty of water

## HONOR RELATIONSHIPS

○ Connect with your partner, a close friend, or a relative

○ Text or call a friend

## MOVE YOUR BEAUTIFUL BODY

○ Stretch in bed

○ Practice gentle yoga or Pilates

## BE KIND TO YOURSELF

○ Shower and brush teeth and hair

○ Open a window, breathe in fresh air, and smile

○ Practice meditation or breathwork

○ Pray, sing, or dance

○ Other: _____

## FEEL YOUR FEELINGS

○ Today I feel _____

## ASK FOR SUPPORT

*Today I could use help with . . .*

○ Holding the baby while I shower or rest

○ Preparing food

○ Laundry and cleaning

○ Other: _____

Today I will ask for help from _____

# DAY 85

Being a mom is hard, and struggling is totally normal. Sharing what's hard can help you digest the burden. Imagine your best friend sitting in front of you. What would you tell them is the hardest part of motherhood right now?

_____

_____

_____

_____

_____

_____

_____

_____

_____

_____

_____

_____

_____

_____

_____

_____

_____

_____

# SELF-CARE CHECKLIST

*Check the ways you've taken care of*
*(or intend to take care of) yourself today:*

## REST DEEPLY

○ Prioritize nighttime sleep

○ Nap when the baby naps at least once a day

## EAT MINDFULLY

○ Nourish yourself with healthy meals and snacks

○ Drink plenty of water

## HONOR RELATIONSHIPS

○ Connect with your partner, a close friend, or a relative

○ Text or call a friend

## MOVE YOUR BEAUTIFUL BODY

○ Stretch in bed

○ Practice gentle yoga or Pilates

## BE KIND TO YOURSELF

○ Shower and brush teeth and hair

○ Open a window, breathe in fresh air, and smile

○ Practice meditation or breathwork

○ Pray, sing, or dance

○ Other: _____

## FEEL YOUR FEELINGS

○ Today I feel _____

## ASK FOR SUPPORT

*Today I could use help with . . .*

○ Holding the baby while I shower or rest

○ Preparing food

○ Laundry and cleaning

○ Other: _____

Today I will ask for help from _____

# DAY 86

Breathe in through your nose, into your heart, and down into your belly. Exhale through your mouth. Repeat for one to five minutes. Afterward, check in with yourself. How did this mindful breathing practice impact your mind, heart, body, and spirit?

_____

_____

_____

_____

_____

_____

_____

_____

_____

_____

_____

_____

_____

_____

_____

_____

_____

# SELF-CARE CHECKLIST

*Check the ways you've taken care of*
*(or intend to take care of) yourself today:*

## REST DEEPLY

○ Prioritize nighttime sleep

○ Nap when the baby naps at least once a day

## EAT MINDFULLY

○ Nourish yourself with healthy meals and snacks

○ Drink plenty of water

## HONOR RELATIONSHIPS

○ Connect with your partner, a close friend, or a relative

○ Text or call a friend

## MOVE YOUR BEAUTIFUL BODY

○ Stretch in bed

○ Practice gentle yoga or Pilates

## BE KIND TO YOURSELF

○ Shower and brush teeth and hair

○ Open a window, breathe in fresh air, and smile

○ Practice meditation or breathwork

○ Pray, sing, or dance

○ Other: _____

## FEEL YOUR FEELINGS

○ Today I feel _____

## ASK FOR SUPPORT

*Today I could use help with . . .*

○ Holding the baby while I shower or rest

○ Preparing food

○ Laundry and cleaning

○ Other: _____

Today I will ask for help from _____

# DAY 87

When you're feeling overwhelmed, it can help to focus all of your attention on just one thing for one full minute. Choose something and observe it with wholehearted curiosity for 60 seconds. How was this practice for you?

_____

_____

_____

_____

_____

_____

_____

_____

_____

_____

_____

_____

_____

_____

_____

_____

_____

_____

_____

_____

# SELF-CARE CHECKLIST

*Check the ways you've taken care of
(or intend to take care of) yourself today:*

## REST DEEPLY

○ Prioritize nighttime sleep

○ Nap when the baby naps at least once a day

## EAT MINDFULLY

○ Nourish yourself with healthy meals and snacks

○ Drink plenty of water

## HONOR RELATIONSHIPS

○ Connect with your partner, a close friend, or a relative

○ Text or call a friend

## MOVE YOUR BEAUTIFUL BODY

○ Stretch in bed

○ Practice gentle yoga or Pilates

## BE KIND TO YOURSELF

○ Shower and brush teeth and hair

○ Open a window, breathe in fresh air, and smile

○ Practice meditation or breathwork

○ Pray, sing, or dance

○ Other: _____

## FEEL YOUR FEELINGS

○ Today I feel _____

## ASK FOR SUPPORT

*Today I could use help with . . .*

○ Holding the baby while I shower or rest

○ Preparing food

○ Laundry and cleaning

○ Other: _____

Today I will ask for help from _____

# DAY 88

Your beautiful body, mind, heart, and spirit are going through a lot of changes right now. Take a moment to check in and cultivate gratitude. Finish these sentences.

Thank you, body, for _____

_____

_____

_____

Thank you, mind, for _____

_____

_____

_____

Thank you, heart, for _____

_____

_____

_____

Thank you, spirit, for _____

_____

_____

_____

# SELF-CARE CHECKLIST

*Check the ways you've taken care of
(or intend to take care of) yourself today:*

## REST DEEPLY

○ Prioritize nighttime sleep

○ Nap when the baby naps at least once a day

## EAT MINDFULLY

○ Nourish yourself with healthy meals and snacks

○ Drink plenty of water

## HONOR RELATIONSHIPS

○ Connect with your partner, a close friend, or a relative

○ Text or call a friend

## MOVE YOUR BEAUTIFUL BODY

○ Stretch in bed

○ Practice gentle yoga or Pilates

## BE KIND TO YOURSELF

○ Shower and brush teeth and hair

○ Open a window, breathe in fresh air, and smile

○ Practice meditation or breathwork

○ Pray, sing, or dance

○ Other: _____

## FEEL YOUR FEELINGS

○ Today I feel _____

## ASK FOR SUPPORT

*Today I could use help with . . .*

○ Holding the baby while I shower or rest

○ Preparing food

○ Laundry and cleaning

○ Other: _____

Today I will ask for help from _____

# DAY 89

Be gentle with yourself as you learn how to do all the things. What are you learning right now? What questions do you have about child-rearing?

_____

_____

_____

_____

_____

_____

_____

_____

_____

_____

_____

_____

_____

_____

_____

_____

_____

_____

# SELF-CARE CHECKLIST

*Check the ways you've taken care of*
*(or intend to take care of) yourself today:*

## REST DEEPLY

○ Prioritize nighttime sleep

○ Nap when the baby naps at least once a day

## EAT MINDFULLY

○ Nourish yourself with healthy meals and snacks

○ Drink plenty of water

## HONOR RELATIONSHIPS

○ Connect with your partner, a close friend, or a relative

○ Text or call a friend

## MOVE YOUR BEAUTIFUL BODY

○ Stretch in bed

○ Practice gentle yoga or Pilates

## BE KIND TO YOURSELF

○ Shower and brush teeth and hair

○ Open a window, breathe in fresh air, and smile

○ Practice meditation or breathwork

○ Pray, sing, or dance

○ Other: _____

## FEEL YOUR FEELINGS

○ Today I feel _____

## ASK FOR SUPPORT

*Today I could use help with . . .*

○ Holding the baby while I shower or rest

○ Preparing food

○ Laundry and cleaning

○ Other: _____

Today I will ask for help from _____

# DAY 90

Make a plan for how you will continue to nurture and support yourself through daily self-care practices. Make a list of your five favorite practices from the past three months and note when and where you will practice.

1. _____

_____

_____

2. _____

_____

_____

3. _____

_____

_____

4. _____

_____

_____

5. _____

_____

_____

# SELF-CARE CHECKLIST

*Check the ways you've taken care of
(or intend to take care of) yourself today:*

## REST DEEPLY

○ Prioritize nighttime sleep

○ Nap when the baby naps at least once a day

## EAT MINDFULLY

○ Nourish yourself with healthy meals and snacks

○ Drink plenty of water

## HONOR RELATIONSHIPS

○ Connect with your partner, a close friend, or a relative

○ Text or call a friend

## MOVE YOUR BEAUTIFUL BODY

○ Stretch in bed

○ Practice gentle yoga or Pilates

## BE KIND TO YOURSELF

○ Shower and brush teeth and hair

○ Open a window, breathe in fresh air, and smile

○ Practice meditation or breathwork

○ Pray, sing, or dance

○ Other: _____

## FEEL YOUR FEELINGS

○ Today I feel _____

## ASK FOR SUPPORT

*Today I could use help with . . .*

○ Holding the baby while I shower or rest

○ Preparing food

○ Laundry and cleaning

○ Other: _____

Today I will ask for help from _____

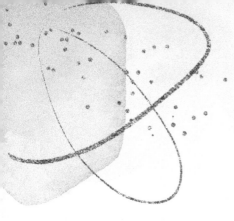

One step at a time. One day at a time.
You are not alone. You got this.

*XO, Kim*

# *Resources*
## FOR FIRST-TIME MOMS

**Aha! Parenting**
Parenting Blog
AhaParenting.com

**Ask Dr. Sears**
Pediatrics, Parenting, and Child Development Resource
AskDrSears.com

**Aviva Romm, MD**
Traditional Wisdom and Modern Medicine for Women
and Children
AvivaRomm.com

**Elizabeth Pantley**
The No-Cry Sleep Solution
NoCrySolution.com

**Every Mother**
Workouts to Prevent and Repair Diastasis Recti
Every-Mother.com

**Glo**
Online Yoga, Meditation, and Pilates Classes
Glo.com

**Hand in Hand Parenting**
Parenting Blog
HandInHandParenting.org

**Insight Timer**
Meditation App
InsightTimer.com

**Janet Lansbury**
Parenting Blog and Podcast
JanetLansbury.com

**Kelly Mom**
Breastfeeding and Parenting Support
KellyMom.com

**Kimberly Ann Johnson**
Postpartum Care Advocate and Author of *The Fourth Trimester*
Magamama.com

**La Leche League International**
Breastfeeding Support
LLLI.org

**Mama Natural**
Pregnancy, Postpartum, and Parenting Blog
MamaNatural.com

**Mother-Baby Behavioral Sleep Lab at the University of Notre Dame**
The Science and Safety of Co-Sleeping
CoSleeping.nd.edu

**Oh Baby Nutrition**
Holistic Nutrition for Mama and Baby
OhBabyNutrition.com

**Postpartum Support International**
Support for Postpartum Depression, Anxiety, and Stress; Online Directory of Maternal Mental Health Professionals
Postpartum.net

**Sanctuary with Rod Stryker**
Meditation and Yoga Nidra App
parayoga.com/sanctuary-meditation-app

**Simplicity Parenting**
Parenting Blog
SimplicityParenting.com

**The Wonder Weeks**
Baby Development App and Book
TheWonderWeeks.com

**Yoga Nidra Network**
Yoga Nidra for New Beginnings
YogaNidraNetwork.org/mp3/yoni-shakti-new-beginnings

# About the Author

**Kim Burris, LMFT,** is a licensed holistic psychotherapist with deep roots in the worlds of yoga, meditation, and mindfulness. She is the founder of The Holistic Counseling Center and received her clinical education and training from the California Institute of Integral Studies. She has lived and practiced at the intersection of psychology and spirituality for over 20 years.

Integrating the depth of Western psychology with the heart and soul of Eastern mysticism, she supports individuals struggling with anxiety, trauma, self-esteem, and motherhood. As a mother of two young boys, she believes that motherhood is a spiritual practice and is passionate about supporting mamas on their journey. Through her counseling practice and online offerings, she helps moms find new ways of being in the world with less stress and more joy.

Kim offers evidence-based treatment with a heart-centered approach that honors the mind, body, and spirit connection. She helps her clients unravel the root cause of their suffering and live from the heart of embodied wisdom. She believes being human is a practice and that healing and change are always possible. You can find her at KimBurris.com.

CPSIA information can be obtained
at www.ICGtesting.com
Printed in the USA
JSHW072358011222
34180JS00001BA/1